Michael G. Faure, Helmut Koziol, Sonja Puntscher-Riekmann (Hg)

# VEREINTES EUROPA – VEREINHEITLICHTES RECHT?

ÖSTERREICHISCHE AKADEMIE DER WISSENSCHAFTEN
PHILOSOPHISCH-HISTORISCHE KLASSE
ZENTRUM SOZIALWISSENSCHAFTEN

---

Sozialwissenschaften im Diskurs

Band 1

ÖSTERREICHISCHE AKADEMIE DER WISSENSCHAFTEN
PHILOSOPHISCH-HISTORISCHE KLASSE
ZENTRUM SOZIALWISSENSCHAFTEN

Michael G. Faure
Helmut Koziol
Sonja Puntscher-Riekmann

# Vereintes Europa – Vereinheitlichtes Recht?

## Die Rechtsvereinheitlichung aus politikwissenschaftlicher, rechtsökonomischer und privatrechtlicher Sicht

Vorgelegt von w. M. HELMUT KOZIOL
in der Sitzung am 14. Dezember 2007

Die verwendete Papiersorte ist aus chlorfrei gebleichtem Zellstoff hergestellt, frei von säurebildenden Bestandsteilen und alterungsbeständig.



ISBN 978-3-7001-6047-2


Druck: Börsedruck Ges.m.b.H., 1230 Wien

http://hw.oeaw.ac.at/6047-2
http://verlag.oeaw.ac.at

# Zentrum Sozialwissenschaften

Das Zentrum Sozialwissenschaften umfasst jene Forschungseinrichtungen, die sich mit den mannigfaltigen Phänomenen des Verhaltens und des gesellschaftlichen Zusammenlebens der Menschen beschäftigen. Die Forschung widmet sich demgemäß neben sozialen Aspekten im engeren Sinn, verschiedenartigen geistes-, kultur- und sogar naturwissenschaftlichen Fragestellungen. Dieses breite Spektrum lenkt den Blick auf oft vernachlässigte Zusammenhänge und erleichtert die Untersuchung von Grenzbereichen und übergreifenden Problemstellungen.

Ein Themenschwerpunkt liegt in den Beziehungen zwischen Mensch und Raum und widmet sich der Dokumentation, Analyse und Interpretation der regionalen, zwischen- und innerstädtischen Disparitäten der Gesellschaft und der Raumnutzung sowie der Bedeutung des globalen Wandels für Gebirgsräume.

Die Entstehung einer supranationalen politischen Gemeinschaft und ihrer Konstitutionalisierung sowie der Analyse von Migrations- und Integrationsprozessen in Österreich und Europa widmet sich ein weiterer Forschungsschwerpunkt. Die interdisziplinäre Anbindung an die internationale Forschung wird dabei durch einen eigenen Schwerpunkt sichergestellt.

Die Beziehung zwischen Mensch und Gesellschaft bilden eine weitere Hauptaufgabe des Zentrums. Es wird das gesellschaftliche Phänomen der Massenmedien und ihre Auswirkung auf die politische Kommunikation in der demokratischen Gesellschaft untersucht. Weitere Projekte beschäftigen sich rechtsvergleichend mit dem für das menschliche Zusammenleben bedeutsamen Schadenersatzrecht, das den Ausgleich erlittener Nachteile regelt und damit auch menschliches Verhalten lenkt.

Schließlich widmet sich ein großer Themenschwerpunkt der Beschreibung, Erklärung und Vorhersage demographischer Prozesse und damit einigen der größten Zukunftsprobleme der modernen westlichen Gesellschaften.

# Vorwort

Die Ende 2006 erfolgte Bildung von Forschungszentren, in denen mehrere Forschungseinrichtungen zusammengefasst werden, hatte nicht zuletzt das Ziel, die fächerübergreifende Forschung zu fördern. Beim Zusammenwirken von Vertretern verschiedener Fachgebiete sollen durch die unterschiedlichen Blickwinkel neue Einsichten für die Beantwortung schon bekannter Fragen gewonnen, aber auch neue Problemstellungen erkannt und diskutiert werden. Der Verwirklichung dieser Ziele dienen unter anderem die Vortragsveranstaltungen, die in unregelmäßigen Abständen vom Zentrum für Sozialwissenschaften veranstaltet werden: Mindestens zwei der Forschungseinrichtungen sollen, allenfalls auch unter Beteiligung von auswärtigen Gästen, ein Thema behandeln.

Die erste derartige Veranstaltung fand am 1. Februar 2007 statt und war einem zwar nicht neuen, aber noch immer höchst aktuellen Thema gewidmet: Der Rechtsvereinheitlichung in einem vereinten Europa. Beteiligt war die Direktorin des Instituts für Europäische Integrationsforschung, der Leiter der Forschungsstelle für Europäisches Schadenersatzrecht und ein Vertreter der ökonomischen Analyse des Rechts, der Professor in Maastricht aber auch Mitarbeiter der eben genannten Forschungsstelle ist. In der allgemeinen Diskussion gehen die Meinungen über die Möglichkeit aber auch die Sinnhaftigkeit einer über das unbedingt nötige Mindestausmaß hinausgehenden Vereinheitlichung weit auseinander. Die Antworten hängen nicht nur, aber unter anderem doch auch davon ab, ob die Frage aus einem politischen, ökonomischen oder rechtstheoretischem Blickwinkel betrachtet wird. Die bisher kaum zu findende Zusammenschau der Ansichten von Vertretern dieser drei unterschiedlichen Fachrichtungen ist geeignet, die Erkenntnis der Einseitigkeit so mancher Argumente und die Erzielung eines ausgewogeneren Standpunktes zu fördern.

Um die Ergebnisse der Veranstaltungen einem größeren Kreis zugänglich zu machen, aber auch um das Zentrum für Sozialwissenschaften stärker im Bewusstsein der Öffentlichkeit zu verankern, haben die Leiter der Forschungseinrichtungen dieses Zentrums beschlossen, die Ergebnisse der Veranstaltungen auch zu veröffentlichen. Mit diesem Bändchen wird eine Reihe im Verlag der Österreichischen Akademie der Wissenschaften eröffnet, in der die gehaltenen Vorträge in etwas erweiterter Form und mit wissenschaftlichen Nachweisen versehen publiziert werden.

Für die Unterstützung bei der Organisation der Veranstaltung und der Erstellung des Manuskriptes sei Herrn Thomas Thiede, LL.B., LL.M. herzlich gedankt.

Wien, im Herbst 2007

*Helmut Koziol*
Zentrumssprecher

# Inhaltsverzeichnis

# Legal Harmonisation from the Perspective of the Economic Analysis of Law

Michael G. Faure*

## *I. Introduction*

In this paper, I address the potential contribution of the economic analysis of law to the debate concerning the need for the harmonisation of private law in Europe. The focus of this paper will indeed mainly be on this harmonisation issue.

Indeed, one way in which an economic analysis can be useful for the study of European integration is that economics has focused a lot of attention on the division of competences within federal systems. This is a topic which, from a European legal perspective, is obviously relevant to the subsidiarity principle. From an economic perspective, the question which is addressed in the economics of federalism is what the optimal level would be for specific types of regulation. In this paper, I argue that this literature is highly useful also for addressing the harmonisation debate with respect to private law. In the paper, I address the desirability of the harmonisation of private law from an economic angle. Economists have indeed paid much attention to the potential goals, functions and economic effects of a harmonisation of law[1].

---

* Institute for Transnational Legal Research (METRO), Maastricht, and Rotterdam Institute for Law and Economics (RKE), Rotterdam, The Netherlands.

[1] This paper builds on earlier research in which harmonisation efforts were analysed from an economic angle with respect to environmental law (Michael Faure, Harmonization of Environmental Law and Market Integration: Harmonizing for the Wrong Reasons?, (1998) European Environmental Law Review (EELR) 169–175), environmental liability (Michael Faure/Kristel De Smedt, Should Europe Harmonise Environmental Liability Legislation?, (2001) Environmental Liability (EL) 217–237), medical malpractice (Michael Faure, Kompensationsmodelle für Heilwesenschäden in Europa mit Ausblick auf die EG – Rechtsharmonisierung, (2000) Zeitschrift für Europäisches Privatrecht (ZEuP) 575–600) and product liability (Michael Faure, Product liability and product safety in Europe: harmonisation or differentiation?, (2000) 53 Kyklos 467–508). See generally Michael Faure, Economic analysis of tort law and the European Civil Code, in: Arthur Hartkamp et al (eds), Towards a European Civil Code, 3rd fully revised and expanded edition, The Hague 2004, 657–676 and Ton Hartlief/Michael Faure, Harmo-

The economics of federalism seems to be a particularly appropriate way of looking at harmonisation efforts in Europe because the European Commission has been using economic arguments to justify its harmonisation efforts for some time. More specifically, the argument has long been advanced that a harmonisation of law, including private law, is necessary in order to harmonise the conditions of competition within Europe. One aspect of this paper is devoted to an analysis of whether this "economic" argument for the harmonisation of the conditions of competition is indeed a valid economic justification for harmonisation. Moreover, applying the economics of federalism to the harmonisation of private law within Europe also has the advantage that a balanced view of the need to harmonise private law can be presented. Indeed, economic analysis does not come up with black or white statements in favour of or against harmonisation, but allows balanced criteria to be advanced on the basis of which those areas and topics which may be good candidates for harmonisation are indicated.

Of course the reader should be aware that applying the economics of federalism to the harmonisation issue means that I will only provide "one view of the cathedral"[2]. Moreover, the harmonisation issue is addressed only from an economic angle in this paper. Although I have argued above that I think economics can provide an interesting contribution to the harmonisation debate, I want to repeat that I realise that this really is just one view of the cathedral. One may indeed well argue that there may be other, non-economic, arguments for a harmonised legal system, such as the belief that this will lead to a higher degree of protection than Member States would achieve when using national law. But even if non-economic arguments are advanced to justify European harmonisation, it seems important, that in future European documents, these reasons are clearly explained within the scope of the subsidiarity principle.

The structure of this paper is as follows: after this introduction (I) a brief insight is provided into the criteria for (de)centralisation in general (II). Then these criteria are applied to private law by focusing more specifically on the reasons for centralisation (III). We then turn to some policy aspects of the harmonisation of private law by addressing it from an interest group perspective (IV) and formulate a few concluding remarks (V).

---

nisatie van aansprakelijkheidsrecht in Europa. Iets over de overlevingskansen van de romantische rechtsschool van Maastricht, in: Ludo Cornelis et al (eds), Liber Amicorum TPR and Marcel Storme, Mechelen 2004, 279–322.

[2] Paraphrasing the words of Calabresi and Melamed (Guido CALABRESI/Douglas MELAMED, Property rules, liability rules and inalienability: one view of the cathedral, (1972) 85 Harvard Law Review (HLR) 1089–1128).

## *II. Starting points for (de)centralisation in general*[3]

### 1. Tiebout

The question of whether regulation should be promulgated at a central (European or federal) level or at a more decentralised level (or, to generalise, what kind of regulation should be set at which level) has been addressed in the economics of federalism. The starting point for the analysis is usually Tiebout's theory about the optimal provision of local public goods[4]. Tiebout argued that when people with the same preferences cluster together in communities, competition between local authorities will, under certain restrictive conditions, lead to allocative efficiency. If there are, for example, in one community citizens who greatly prefer sporting facilities and in another a majority of citizens with a preference for opera, the first community will probably construct sporting facilities, whereas the second may build an opera house. If someone living in the second community preferred sporting facilities to the opera house, he could then move to the first community, which apparently provides services more to his tastes. The idea is that well-informed citizens will move to the community that provides the local services that are best adapted to their personal preferences. Through this so-called «voting with the feet», competition between local authorities will lead citizens to cluster together according to their preferences[5]. In practice, it is clear that different communities do indeed offer a variety of different services. The idea is that the citizen can have an effect on this provision of local public goods either by influencing the decision-making (vote) or by moving (exit).

---

[3] This part of the paper is largely based on the inauguration address of Roger Van den Bergh, in which the economic literature of the criteria for (de)centralisation is discussed (Roger VAN DEN BERGH, Subsidiariteit rechtseconomisch bekeken. Adieu Bruxelles?, Arnhem 1994. An English summary of this inauguration address has been published by Roger VAN DEN BERGH, The Subsidiarity Principle in European Community Law, (1994) Maastricht Journal of European and Comparative Law (MJ) 337). See also Roger VAN DEN BERGH, Towards an Institutional Legal Framework for Regulatory Competition in Europe, (2000) 53 Kyklos 435–466.

[4] Charles M. TIEBOUT, A Pure Theory of Local Expenditures, (1956) Journal of Policital Economy (JPE) 416. For a discussion, see Susan ROSE-ACKERMAN, Rethinking the Progressive Agenda, the Reform of the American Regulatory State, New York 1992, 169–170.

[5] Compare Dennis C. MUELLER, Federalism and the European Union: A Constitutional Perspective, (1997) 90 Public Choice (PC) 255–280.

## 2. Competing legal orders

This basic idea applies not only to community services, but also, for example, to fiscal decisions[6] and environmental choices[7]. In addition, this idea of citizens moving to the community that provides services which best correspond with their preferences can also be applied with respect to legal rules. Thus, it has been argued by Van den Bergh that competition between legislators will lead to legal systems competing with each other to provide the legislation that corresponds best to the preferences of citizens. Ogus also argues that the various lawmakers in the nation states will create a competitive market for the supply of law[8]. The idea therefore is that in an optimal world, citizens will cluster together in states that provide legal rules that correspond to their preferences. Well-informed citizens who are dissatisfied with the legislation provided could move (voting with the feet) to the community that provides legislation that corresponds best to their preferences. This idea, assuming that different legal systems offer different legal rules to satisfy the demands of the citizens, thus explains the variety and differences between legal systems[9]. Moreover, it also shows that differences between the various legal rules of different countries should not necessarily be judged negatively, as is often the case in Europe today. The idea of competing legal systems can probably best be seen "in action" in private international law where actors can choose the legal system that best suits their needs in a choice of law regime[10]. Frey and Eichenberger have proposed an extreme form of this competition between legal orders by suggesting the emergence of Functional Overlapping Competing Jurisdictions (FOCJ), whereby citi-

---

[6] See, eg, Robert INMAN/Daniel RUBINFELD, The EMU and Fiscal Policy in the New European Community: An Issue for Economic Federalism, (1994) International Review of Law and Economics (IRLE) 147.

[7] Thus, Wallace OATES/Robert SCHWAB, Economic Competition among Jurisdictions: Efficiency Enhancing or Distortion Inducing?, (1988) 35 Journal of Public Economics 333–354.

[8] Anthony OGUS, Competition between National Legal Systems: A Contribution to Economic Analysis to Comparative Law, (1999) ICLQ 405–418, and see Anthony OGUS, The Contribution of Economic Analysis of Law to Legal Transplant, in: Jan SMITS (ed), The Contribution of Mixed Legal Systems to European Law, Antwerp 2001, 27–37.

[9] Roger VAN DEN BERGH, (1998) MJ 134 and Roger VAN DEN BERGH, (2000) 53 Kyklos 437–439.

[10] Although the choice for a particular legal regime may not always be related to the quality of the legal system but, say, to the quality of the court or arbitration system. The latter explains, according to Ogus, the popularity of English law in choice of law clauses in contracts (Anthony OGUS, (1999) ICLQ 408).

zens could choose different governmental authorities for different functions of government[11].

Obviously, this system, assuming that competition between legal orders leads to allocative efficiency in the provision of legal rules, works only if certain conditions are met. One condition is that citizens have adequate information on the contents of the legal rules provided by the various legislators in order to be able to make an informed choice. In addition, exit is often costly, so people may stay even if the (legal) regime does not best suit their needs[12]. Moreover, a location decision is obviously made under the influence of a set of criteria, in which the legal regime may not be decisive[13]. Usually job location and residence are so important that in reality there is little left for people to choose[14]. Finally, as we will discuss below, this system of competition between legal orders works only if the decisions in one legal order have no external effects on others.

### 3. "Bottom up federalism"

In economic literature, the Tiebout model is used to argue that, from an economic point of view, decentralisation should be the starting point, since competition between legislators will lead to allocative efficiency. Van den Bergh also uses his theory to provide criteria for centralisation/decentralisation within the European Union. Taking Tiebout as a starting point and assuming that competition between decentralised legislators will lead to an optimal provision of legal rules, the crucial question is: why centralise? Van den Bergh criticises the fact that part of the current discussion in European legal literature seems to focus on the question of why there should be decentralisation (referred to by Van den Bergh as 'top down federalisation'). According to economic theory, that is the wrong question. Proceeding from

---

[11] Bruno Frey, FOCJ: Competitive Governments for Europe, (1996) IRLE 315–327, see also Bruno Frey/Reiner Eichenberger, To Harmonise or to Compete? That's Not the Question, (1996) Journal of Public Economics 335 and Alessandra Casella/Bruno Frey, Federalism and clubs. Towards an Economic Theory of Overlapping Political Jurisdiction, (1992) European Economic Review (EER) 639.

[12] As Ogus states, there should be no barriers to the freedom of establishment and to the movement of capital (Anthony Ogus, (1999) ICLQ 407). For these conditions, see also Roger Van den Bergh, (2000) 53 Kyklos 438.

[13] That is one of the reasons why Frey and Eichenberger argue in favour of FOCJ: the choice for one legal or institutional regime should not be exclusive; there may be 'overlapping' jurisdictions depending upon the different functions (Bruno Frey/Reiner Eichenberger, (1996) Journal of Public Economics 316–318).

[14] Susan Rose-Ackerman (supra fn 4) 169.

Tiebout's model, there is reason to believe in what Van den Bergh calls a "bottom up federalisation", assuming that in principle the local level is optimal, since the local level has the best information on local problems and on the preferences of citizens. Decision making should be moved to a higher level only when there is a good reason[15]. Economic theory has indeed suggested that there may be a variety of reasons why the local level is not best suited to take decisions and that there are occasions when central decision making can lead to more efficient results.

I will now apply these criteria for centralisation and relate them to the harmonisation of private law in Europe.

## *III. The criteria for centralisation of tort law*

### 1. The transboundary character of the externality

The Tiebout argument in favour of competition between local communities obviously works only if the problem to be regulated is indeed merely local. Once it has been established that the problem to be regulated has a transboundary character, there may be arguments to be made in favour of centralisation. First, there is an economies of scale argument to shift powers to a higher legal order that has competence to deal with the externality over a larger territory. This corresponds with the basic insight that if the problem to be regulated crosses the borders of competence of the regulatory authority, the decision-making power should be shifted to a higher regulatory level, preferably to an authority which has jurisdiction over a territory large enough to deal with the problem adequately[16]. "Economic theory provides a straightforward but unrealistic answer to regional problems: draw 'optimal' jurisdictional boundaries"[17]. This "economies of scale" argument is thus related to the argument that transaction costs will be lower if regula-

---

[15] A major American supporter of this "presumption in favour of decentralisation" is Revesz. See, eg, Richard REVESZ, Environmental Regulation in Federal Systems, in: Han SOMSEN (ed.), Yearbook of European Environmental Law, Oxford 2000, 1–35 and Richard REVESZ, Federalism and Environmental Regulation: An Overview, in: Richard REVESZ/Philippe SANDS/Richard STEWART (eds), Environmental Law: The Economy and Sustainable Development, Cambridge 2000, 37–79.

[16] Compare: Anthony OGUS, (1999) ICLQ 414 and Cliona KIMBER, A Comparison of Environmental Federalism in the United States and The European Union, (1995) 54 Maryland Law Review (MaLR) 1; Dan ESTY, Revitalizing Environmental Federalism, (1996) 95 Michigan Law Review (MiLR) 625; and Susan ROSE-ACKERMAN (supra fn 4) 164–165.

[17] Thus, Susan ROSE-ACKERMAN, Controlling Environmental Pollution: The Limits of Public Law in Germany and the United States, New Haven 1995, 38.

tion is made at the higher level[18]. There is, however, another argument in favour of centralisation which relates to the fact that in cases of transboundary externalities, states would have no incentive to impose stringent regulations upon their own citizens if the consequences of harmful actions were only felt outside their own territories. Transboundary externalities may thus create inefficiencies in the absence of central regulation[19].

This argument in favour of centralisation could thus play a role with respect to transboundary torts. Thus, many have proposed central decision making in the area of environmental liability, since this area of private law is typically transboundary. However, this externality argument obviously cannot provide a general justification for the harmonisation of rules of tort law as long as accidents are confined within national borders. Moreover, even with these typical transboundary torts one should not move too hastily to centralisation, since there may be remedies within national law which are as effective in dealing with these transboundary problems.

Moreover, Van den Bergh has demonstrated that in some cases, more particularly in the area of private law, European law cannot be considered an effective remedy to the interstate externality problem[20]. In some cases, European law goes further than is necessary to cure transboundary externalities; in other cases legal instruments less comprehensive than total harmonisation could be used to remedy the problem[21]. There is, in other words, always the risk that the cure may be worse than the disease. The first issue relates to the fact that European Directives often cover both local and community-wide problems, such as pollution, without making a distinction between regional and interstate pollution[22]. The second point is that in some cases transboundary externalities may also be internalised by national law. The simple fact of transboundary effects is therefore not sufficient to justify European law-making[23]. Nevertheless, there certainly may be cases where one could hold that decentralised legal rule making would not be able to remedy the transboundary externality.

This shows indeed that in cases of transboundary torts there may be an argument in favour of centralisation, but only if there is indeed a serious risk

---

[18] It is thus related to the 'transaction cost' argument, to be discussed below.

[19] See, for the 'interstate externalities' and 'economies of scale' justifications for centralisation, Richard REVESZ (supra fn 15) 67.

[20] Roger VAN DEN BERGH, (1998) MJ 143.

[21] Roger VAN DEN BERGH, (1998) MJ 144–145.

[22] Thus, Roger VAN DEN BERGH, Economics in a Legal Strait-Jacket: The Difficult Reception of Economic Analysis in European Law, paper presented at the workshop Empirical Research and Legal Realism: Setting the Agenda, Haifa, 6–9 June 1999, 10.

[23] Roger VAN DEN BERGH, (1998) MJ 144–145.

that nation states would be able to externalise harm, in other words if the nation states were able to shift the negative effects of their own actions onto the shoulders of their neighbours. Moreover, European harmonisation would then have to be limited to transboundary torts. The transboundary externality argument indeed provides no justification for a harmonisation of tort law that merely deals with "national torts". Finally, it would have to be clear that national legal remedies cannot provide an adequate answer to the problem posed by interstate torts.

## 2. The race for the bottom

*a) General: the risk of destructive competition*

There may be an economic argument for centralisation in that there is a risk that a "race for the bottom" would emerge between countries to attract foreign investments. As a result of this, prisoner's dilemmas could arise, whereby countries would fail to enact or enforce effective legislation. Centralisation can be advanced as a remedy for these prisoner's dilemmas. This race-for-the-bottom argument could in theory play a role in the case of product safety as well[24]. It would mean that local governments would compete against each other with lenient environmental legislation to attract industry[25]. The result would be an overall reduction of environmental quality below efficient levels. This would correspond with the traditional game theory result that prisoner's dilemmas create inefficiencies.

The race-for-the-bottom argument has had supporters as well as opponents in North American scholarship. Law and economics scholars tend to stress the benefits of competition between states and point out the dangers of centralisation[26], whereas some legal scholars tend to attach more belief to the race-for-the-bottom rationale for centralisation[27].

---

[24] For a detailed discussion of this argument, see Dan ESTY/Damien GERADIN, Environmental Protection Policies and International Competitiveness: A Conceptual Framework, (1998) Journal of World Trade (JWT) 16–19.

[25] Compare Susan ROSE-ACKERMAN (supra fn 4) 166–170.

[26] See Richard REVESZ, Rehabilitating Interstate Competition: Rethinking the Race for the Bottom Rationale for Federal Environmental Regulation, (1992) New York University Law Review (NYULR) 1210–1254 and Richard REVESZ, Federalism and Interstate Environmental Externalities, (1996) University of Pennsylvania Law Review (UPLR) 2341–2416.

[27] See Dan ESTY/Damien GERADIN, Market Access, Competitiveness, and Harmonization: Environmental Protection in Regional Trade Agreements, (1997) 21 Harvard Environmental Law Review (HELR) 265–336 and (1998) 32/3 JWT 5–46.

As we will indicate below, this race-for-the-bottom argument has not as such been explicitly discussed in the European legal debate. It only shows up in the argument that the conditions of competition should be harmonised. That will be discussed below. From an economic perspective, the race for the bottom is only a rationale for centralisation if it can be established that states could attract industry with lenient tort rules[28]. Let us examine, on the basis of an example, whether that is a realistic scenario.

*b) Example: environmental liability*

From an economic perspective, differences in the conditions of competition only pose a problem if it is clear that environmental costs would be considerably different between the Member States and that these differences would lead to the relocation of firms to the Member States with the lowest standards. In that case, the so-called race-for-the-bottom argument, referred to as the "pollution haven" hypothesis in environmental cases, might be an argument in favour of centralisation [29]. The question therefore arises as to whether there is empirical evidence that states can indeed attract industry with lenient environmental standards.

Empirical evidence to uphold this race-for-the-bottom rationale is rather weak. Repetto argues that pollution control costs are only a minor fraction of the total sales in manufacturing industries[30]. Moreover, Jaffe/Peterson/Portney/Stavins[31] argue that empirical evidence shows that the effects of environmental regulations are "either small, statistically insignificant or not robust to tests of model specification". They argue that the stringency of environmental regulations might have some effect on new firms in their decision to locate for the first time[32], but that this will not induce existing firms to relocate. They equally argue that other criteria such as tax levels, public services and the unionisation of the labour force have a much more significant impact on the location decision than environmental regulation.

---

[28] See Roger VAN DEN BERGH, (2000) 53 Kyklos 445.

[29] Although Esty and Geradin have rightly pointed out the fact that a whole variety of legal instruments exists which might remedy the problem, whereby the total harmonisation of standards would be the most far-reaching (Dan ESTY/Damien GERADIN, (1997) 21 HELR 282–294).

[30] Robert REPETTO, Trade and Sustainable Development, UNEP, Environment and Trade Series, Geneva 1994.

[31] Adam JAFFE/Steven PETERSON/Paul PORTNEY/Robert STAVINS, Environmental Regulation and the Competitiveness of US Manufacturing: What Does the Evidence Tell Us?, (1995) 33 Journal of Economic Literature (JEL) 132–163.

[32] See Dan ESTY/Damien GERADIN, (1998) 32/3 JWT 12–15.

Recently, this empirical evidence has been somewhat contradicted by Xing/Kolstad[33], who argue that the laxity of environmental regulations in a host country is a significant determinant of foreign direct investment by the US chemical industry. The more lax the regulations, the more likely the country is to attract foreign investment, so Xing/Kolstad argue. Although this somewhat weakens the evidence presented by Jaffe/Peterson/Portney/Stavins as far as the location of new firms outside the US is concerned, it does not contradict their finding that existing firms will not relocate solely because of the stringency of environmental regulations.

Arguments against the race-for-the-bottom rationale for central environmental regulation have also been formulated with respect to the American example. Many scholars[34], among them Revesz[35] in particular, have argued that this race-for-the-bottom argument finds no support in existing models of interjurisdictional competition.[36] In addition, Revesz stresses that central standard-setting would not be an effective response to the race-for-the-bottom problem, since the local communities concerned would have other means to attract industry if they wish (relaxation of regulatory controls in other areas). Revesz has encountered opposition, especially from Esty[37], but he has provided a powerful reply to his critics[38].

This material, therefore, weakens the prisoner's dilemma argument. Moreover, it has also been argued that as far as environmental standards are concerned, it is not at all clear that there will be a race for the bottom. There is also some evidence that Member States do in fact strive for high environmental standards, even if this imposes extra costs or burdens on their industries. Some countries may therefore be more involved in a race for the

---

33 Yuqing XING/Charles D. KOLSTAD, Do Lax Environmental Regulations Attract Foreign Investment, 16–95 (Working Paper in Economics, University of California 1995).

34 See eg Sam PELZMAN/T. TIDEMAN, Local v. National Pollution Control: Note, (1972) American Economic Review (AER) 959–963 and E. Donald ELLIOTT/Bruce ACKERMAN/John MILLIAN, Towards a Theory of Statutory Evolution: The Federalization of Environmental Law, (1985) Journal of Law, Economics & Organization (JLEO) 313–340.

35 Richard REVESZ, (1992) NYULR 1210–1254 and Richard REVESZ, (1996) UPLR 2341–2416.

36 See for a similar conclusion with respect to natural resource legislation Jason S. JOHNSTON, The tragedy of centralisation: the political economics of American natural resource federalism, (2003) vol 74 University of Colorado Law Review 487–649, who argues that regulatory centralisation may be just as tragic for natural resources as the regime of local control that it is designed to replace.

37 Dan ESTY, (1996) 95 MiLR 570–653.

38 Richard REVESZ, The Race for the Bottom and Federal Environmental Regulation: A Response to Critics, (1997) Minnesota Law Review (MinLR) 535–564.

top instead of a race for the bottom[39]. One could also question whether European law is at all able to remedy a real race-for-the-bottom risk, given the enforcement deficit.

## 3. Harmonisation of marketing conditions

*a) General*

This race-for-the-bottom argument, that competition among jurisdictions for economic activity will be "destructive", corresponds – to some extent – with the European legal argument that the creation of harmonised conditions of competition is necessary to avoid trade distortions. This argument was traditionally used to support harmonisation of Member States' legislation in a variety of areas. Simply stated, the argument is that complying with legislation imposes costs on industry. If legislation is different, these costs would therefore differ as well and the conditions of competition within the common market would not be equal. The argument apparently assumes that total equality of conditions of competition is necessary for the functioning of the common market. "Levelling the playing field" for European industry is the central message.

There are, however, some problems with this traditional European argument which in fact claims that any difference in legislation between the Member States might endanger the conditions of competition and therefore justifies harmonisation of legal rules. The latter argument seems particularly weak[40]. From an economic point of view, the mere fact that conditions of competition differ does not necessarily create a race-for-the-bottom risk. There can be differences in marketing conditions for a variety of reasons, and if the conditions of competition were indeed totally equal, as the argument assumes, there would also be no trade.

Also, Europe has developed an elaborate set of rules which guarantee – *inter alia* – a free flow of products and services[41] and thus contribute to

---

[39] Thus, Roger VAN DEN BERGH/Michael FAURE/Jürgen LEFEVERE, The Subsidiarity Principle in European Environmental Law: An Economic Analysis, in: Erling EIDE/Roger VAN DEN BERGH (eds), Law and Economics of the Environment, Oslo 1996, 141–142. Ogus argues that firms may benefit from being located in a high standard Member State, since this may generate technological improvements and thus competitive advantages; that may explain the race for the top (Anthony OGUS, (1999) 48 ICLQ 415). See, generally, David VOGEL, Trading Up: Consumer and Environmental Regulation in the Global Economy, Cambridge 1995, 13–14.

[40] See also Jaap SPIER/Olav A. HAAZEN, The European Group on Tort Law ("Tilburg Group") and the European Principles of Tort Law, (1999) ZEuP 478.

[41] See articles 28–30 of the Treaty (the "old" articles 30–36).

market integration without necessitating the harmonisation of all rules and standards[42]. In this context, the case law of the European Court of Justice with respect to the free movement of goods versus environmental protection springs to mind. This shows that the goal of market integration can be achieved through (other) instruments less comprehensive than total harmonisation[43], which can remove barriers to trade just as effectively. Hence, one should make a distinction between the political ideal of creating one common market in Europe on the one hand and the (economic) race-for-the-bottom argument on the other hand[44].

This political goal of market integration may be questioned on economic grounds[45] and may justify the need for rules aiming at a reduction of trade restrictions such as, for example, the harmonisation of product standards. The problem is that initiatives such as those in the area of environmental law also aim at the harmonisation of process standards "to harmonise conditions of competition". That seems questionable on efficiency grounds[46].

It should be stressed that the European argument that markets will be distorted unless the conditions of competition are harmonised is not only constantly repeated in a stereotypical way, but its validity is hardly ever questioned. The argument as it is usually presented in Europe, cannot, as was stated above, be fitted into the economic criteria for centralisation, since it suggests that the removal of every difference in legal systems would be necessary to cure the race-for-the-bottom risk; this is neither supported by economic theory, nor by empirical evidence. Also even if one were to take the (political) "common market" goal as a starting point and private law were to be harmonised on that ground, this would still not create a level playing field since differences in, for example, energy sources, access to raw materials and atmospheric conditions will still lead to marketing conditions that favour trade[47].

There is, in addition, a strong counter-argument: there are many examples showing that economic market integration is possible (without the distortions

---

42 See generally on the potential conflict between free trade and environmental protection, Dan ESTY, Economic Integration and the Environment, in: Norman VIG/Regina AXELROD (eds), The Global Environment: institutions, law and policy, Washington 1999, 190–209.

43 See also Dan ESTY/Damien GERADIN, (1997) HELR 296–299 and Anthony OGUS, Regulation, Legal Form and Economic Theory, Oxford 1994, 177–179.

44 See also Richard Revesz, who likewise argues that these are separate points which should be distinguished (Richard REVESZ (supra fn 26) 19).

45 See Roger VAN DEN BERGH (supra fn 22).

46 This is also criticized by Richard REVESZ (supra fn 26) 19.

47 Thus, Roger VAN DEN BERGH (supra fn 22) 6.

predicted by the race-for-the-bottom argument) with non-standardised legal orders. Public choice scholars have often advanced the Swiss federal model as an example of where economic market integration goes hand in hand with differentiated legal systems[48]. It is apparently possible to create a common market without the total harmonisation of all legal rules and standards. That is not to say that there may not be other arguments in favour of the harmonization of tort law in Switzerland. Notably the reduction-of-transaction-costs argument – to be discussed below – may well constitute a powerful reason to prefer one federal Swiss tort law instead of 26 different cantonal systems. Therefore, clear steps towards harmonisation of private law can be seen in Switzerland as well[49]. Note, however, that this is not because harmonisation would be necessary to make market integration possible.

*b) Example: product liability*

The harmonisation of the conditions of competition argument has obviously played an important role in the area of product liability and, it has even been used explicitly as (one of the) rationales for the European Product Liability Directive. In the product liability debate, the traditional argument that uniform rules in Europe are necessary to guarantee the free movement of goods within the EC was often heard. What can be said about this argument?

A distinction should probably be made in this respect between product safety standards on the one hand and product liability rules on the other hand. It could be argued that differences in product safety standards may indeed endanger interstate trade. Therefore rules with respect to – *inter alia* – a free flow of products and services may certainly contribute to the European goal of market integration. The Product Safety Directive 52/59 of 29 June 1992 clearly aims at removing differences in safety standards, since the Commission considers that these differences might endanger the establishment of the internal market. The preamble reads:

> "Whereas it is important to adopt measures with the aim of progressively establishing the internal market over a period expiring on 31 December 1992; whereas the internal market is to comprise an area without internal frontiers in which the free movement of goods, persons, services and capital is ensured;

---

48 Bruno FREY, Direct Democracy: Politico-Economic Lessons from Switzerland, (1994) AER 338–342.

49 See Bénedict WININGER, L'architecture de l'Avant-projet de loi sur la responsabilité civile, (2001) Revue de Droit Suisse (RDS) 299–326; and Helmut KOZIOL, Das Niederländische BW unter der Schweizer Entwurf als Vorbildes für ein künftiges europäisches Schadenersatzrecht, (1996) ZEuP 592–593.

> Whereas some Member States have adopted horizontal legislation on product safety, imposing in particular, a general obligation on economic operators to market only safe products;
> Whereas those legislations differ in the level of protection afforded to persons;
> Whereas such disparities and the absence of horizontal legislation in other Member States are liable to create barriers to trade and distortions of competition within the internal market."

Where the preamble to the Directive of 29 June 1992 on general product safety therefore clearly states that disparities and the absence of horizontal legislation in other Member States are liable to create barriers to trade and distortions of competition within the internal market, this is probably true. However, the question arises as to whether the goal of market integration can only be achieved by means of such a comprehensive instrument as total harmonisation and more particularly the question arises as to whether this may justify the harmonisation of rules of private law, such as product liability. Indeed, the political goal of market integration may justify some rules aiming at the reduction of trade restrictions (think about the case law of the European Court of Justice with respect to the free movement of goods) and may justify a minimum harmonisation of product safety standards. In that respect the directive on general product safety in fact only provides for a general obligation to place only safe products on the market, but safety standards may still be drawn up in the Member State in which the product is in circulation or may rely on codes of good practice, which need not necessarily be European[50].

Ogus is relatively enthusiastic about these product safety directives, precisely because the harmonisation is limited to "essential safety requirements". To meet these requirements the Member States can still use their national standards, whereby voluntary standards set by expert committees will allow for easy mutual recognition. The approach chosen in the product safety directives therefore actually promotes competition between different national and European standards systems, so Ogus holds[51].

The goal of "levelling the playing field" is much more apparent in the Product Liability Directive. That directive is clearly justified on the ground that differing liability rules in the Member States would hamper the conditions of competition. The considerations preceding the directive read:

> "Whereas approximation of the laws of the Member States concerning the liability of the producer for damage caused by the defectiveness of his products is necessary because the existing divergences may distort competition and affect the movement of goods within the common market".

[50] See article 4 (2) of the Directive 92/59 of 29 June 1992 on general product safety.

[51] Anthony OGUS (supra fn 43) 177–179.

The weakness of this argument is that it assumes that differences in marketing conditions are always and necessarily a problem for the creation of a common market. Conditions of competition are obviously never equal, as the levelling-the-playing-field argument assumes. In the ideal case of totally equal market conditions, there would be no trade. This political goal of market integration may moreover be questioned on economic grounds[52]. In addition one should realise that, even if product liability law were totally harmonised in Europe, this would still not create a level playing field, since differences in, for example, energy sources, access to raw materials and atmospheric conditions will still lead to market conditions that distort trade[53].

There is, in addition, a strong counter-argument, in that there are many examples showing that economic market integration is possible (without the distortions predicted by the race-for-the-bottom argument) with differentiated legal orders. Public choice scholars have often advanced the above-mentioned Swiss federal model as an example where economic market integration goes hand in hand with differentiated legal systems[54]. It is apparently possible to create a common market without total harmonisation of all legal rules and standards[55].

Finally, it may be questioned whether the European Product Liability Directive, as drafted, can indeed achieve a total harmonisation of marketing conditions. It is in fact very unlikely that this is the case[56]. Indeed, according to article 13, all the different, already existing, product liability laws remain in effect, which means differences that already exist will remain unchanged. In addition, the directive itself refers to national legislation at many points, for example, with respect to the rights of contribution or recourse (article 5 and 8.1), with respect to non-material damage (article 9), the suspension or interruption of the limitation period (article 10.2) and with respect to nuclear accidents (article 14). It should also be mentioned that in

[52] See for a critical analysis Roger Van den Bergh (supra fn 22).

[53] Thus, Roger Van den Bergh (supra fn 22) 6.

[54] Bruno Frey, (1994) AER 338–342.

[55] See equally Richard Revesz, Federalism and Environmental Regulation: lessons for the European Union and the International Community, (1997) Virginia Law Review (VLR) 1338–1341.

[56] Almost all authors agree on that point. See Harry Duintjer Tebbens, De Europese Richtlijn Produktaansprakelijkheid, (1986) Nederlands Juristenblad (NJB) 373–374; P. Storm, Een gebrekkig produkt, (1985) Maandblad voor Ondernemingsrecht (TVVS) 245; Arent J.O. Van Wassenaer van Catwijck, Produktaansprakelijkheid, in: Serie Praktijkhandleidingen, Zwolle 1986, 81 and Miquel Martin Casals/José Solé Feliu, Responsabilidad por productas en España y (des)armonizacion Europea, (2001) 4 Revista de responsabilidad civil y seguros 1–17.

three cases the directive expressly allows the Member States to derogate from the provisions of the directive – namely liability for primary agricultural products, liability for development risks and the introduction of a financial limit on liability. Moreover, the directive cannot of course bring any harmonisation for all the product accidents to which it does not apply, because of limitations in the definitions of "product", "producer" and "damage". Many notions in the directive are also unclear and can give rise to interpretation problems[57]. These problems might lead to different interpretations of the provisions of the directive by the legislator and courts of the different Member States. These interpretation problems can be solved by the European Court of Justice in Luxembourg. But it often takes a long time before an interpretation problem is brought before the Court and as long as there is no definitive solution, these interpretation problems of unclear notions in the directive might again endanger the harmonisation objective. Interpretational problems are all the more likely in practice since even the language differences of the various translations of the directive can lead to different interpretations of the same provision[58]. It has already been mentioned that the Product Liability Directive gave several options to the Member States, concerning primary agricultural products, the liability for development risks and the possibility of introducing a financial limit on liability. Obviously, this has also caused differences, as we just indicated. These differences, as far as the writing of the directive into domestic law is concerned, are shown in annex 1 to the Green Paper on liability for defective products[59].

Since it is clear that this Product Liability Directive cannot approximate the Member State's legislation, it has been suggested that this could only be used as an argument to give the EC competence in this matter[60]. For

[57] Consider the defect notion in article 6, which might have different interpretations.

[58] See for instance the different meaning of the "lower threshold" in article 9 in the French and the Dutch versions. Another example is that in the English text producer liability is called "liability without fault", whereas in the Dutch version it is just "liability". For other examples see Michael FAURE/Willy VANBUGGENHOUT, Produktaansprakelijkheid. De Europese richtlijn: harmonisatie en consumentenbescherming, (1987–88) Rechtskundig Weekblad (RW) 1–14 and 33–49.

[59] Green Paper on Liability for Defective Products, COM (1999) 396 final.

[60] Article 100 of the EEC treaty indeed gave legislative competence to the Community to harmonize the different legislations of the Member States. It was, however, heavily debated whether this article 100 was an appropriate basis on which to ground the legislative power of the EC with respect to product liability (see Ludwig KRÄMER, EEC Consumer Law, in: Ludwig KRÄMER, Droit et Consommation, The Hague-New York 1986, 274–275).

all these reasons some authors qualify the directive itself as a defective product[61].

From this it follows that the Product Liability Directive still relies heavily on national law and can for that reason never lead to a "levelling of the playing field" or a "harmonisation of marketing conditions". This example of the European Product Liability Directive therefore nicely shows that the harmonisation of the conditions of competition argument is not a useful basis for European action towards centralisation.

### 4. Reduction of transaction costs

*a) General*

There may, however, be one final economic argument in favour of harmonisation, based on the reduction of transaction costs. This argument is often advanced by European legal scholars pleading for harmonisation of private law in Europe, and is based on the belief that differences in legal systems are very complex and only serve Brussels law firms[62]. This argument cannot be examined in detail here[63]. It is obviously too simplistic to claim that a harmonised legal system is always more efficient than differentiated legal rules because of the transaction cost savings inherent in harmonised rules[64]. Such argument neglects the fact that there are substantial benefits from differentiation whereby legislation can be adapted to the preferences of individuals[65]. Moreover, given the differences between the legal systems (and legal cultures) in Europe, the costs of harmonisation may also be huge – if not prohibitive[66]. The crucial question therefore is whether the possible transaction cost

---

61 This is the title of an article by P. Storm, (1985) TVVS 241–246.

62 This is one of the arguments made by the Danish scholar Lando in favour of harmonised private law. Ole Lando, Die Regeln des Europäischen Vertragsrecht, in: Peter-Christian Müller-Graff (ed), Gemeinsames Privatrecht in der Europäischen Gemeinschaft, Baden-Baden 1993, 473–474. See also on the costs of a differentiated European contract law the contributions in Stefan Vogenauer/Stephen Weatherhill (eds), The harmonisation of European contract law. Implications for European private laws, business and legal practice, Oxford 2000, and in Fabrizio Cafaggi (ed), The institutional framework of European private law, Oxford 2006.

63 It is further developed and criticised by Roger Van den Bergh, (1998) MJ 129–152.

64 Compare Susan Rose-Ackerman (supra fn 4) 172, who argues that uniform federal regulation may reduce search costs and tends to produce a more stable and predictable jurisprudence.

65 See, for the environmental case, R. Mendelsohn, Regulatory Heterogeneous Emissions, (1986) Journal of Environmental Economics and Management (JEEM) 301.

66 That point has especially been made by Pierre Legrand, The impossibility of legal transplants, (1997) MJ 111.

savings of harmonisation outweigh the benefits of differentiated legal rules. There is little empirical evidence to support the statement that transaction cost savings could justify European harmonisation of all kinds of legal rules. Moreover, the transaction cost savings are likely to be relatively small[67].

However, this reduction of transaction cost argument is probably the most important justification for several initiatives (mostly at the private academic level) that have been taken towards a harmonisation of tort law. The crucial question in that respect is obviously whether differences between legal systems are, as Legrand for one suggests, so heavily rooted in legal culture and legal tradition that they should be considered as reflecting differing preferences of the citizens or whether they merely concern pointless incompatibilities that do not reflect differences in value patterns at all. Again, one needs to differentiate here between the various areas of private law under consideration. If it were possible, for example, to establish that in fact in most European legal systems strict liability is only used for hazardous activities and activities related to such and that basically a fault/negligence regime still applies to non-hazardous activities, then one could argue that there are differing formulations of the strict liability rule, but that the citizens apparently have similar preference patterns[68]. Such a legal issue, like the question of when strict liability could be introduced, would thus be a good candidate for harmonisation on the basis of the transaction cost reduction. But again, it would still be necessary to examine whether the differences in the legal techniques used in the various legal systems to describe the strict liability regimes could indeed be bridged at relatively low costs.[69] Otherwise, the marginal costs of harmonisation may once again be higher than the benefits. Indeed, as was mentioned above, it is relatively difficult to argue that there are any benefits at all, other than that it would be easier for lawyers from various Member States to deal with tort rules in other Member States. But, given the (probably relatively low) benefit of harmonisation, the

---

[67] Thus, Roger VAN DEN BERGH, (1998) MJ 146–148.

[68] I am certainly not arguing that this would indeed be the case. The experiences of the various "harmonisation groups" have demonstrated precisely that considerable differences still exist as far as the scope of application of strict liability regimes is concerned. See eg Bernhard A. KOCH/Helmut KOZIOL (eds), Unification of Tort Law, Strict Liability, The Hague-London-New York 2002.

[69] For an overview of the differences see inter alia Cees VAN DAM, European Tort Law, Oxford 2006, Walter VAN GERVEN/Jeremy LEVER/Pierre LAROUCHE, Tort Law Scope of Protection – Cases, Materials and Texts on National, Supranational and International Tort Law, Oxford 2000, and Franz WERRO/Vernon PALMER (eds), The boundaries of strict liability in European tort law, Durham (North Carolina) Bern-Bruxelles 2004.

costs of harmonisation should therefore be even lower, which obviously is questionable.

However, if it were possible (also with the use of law and economics) to show that differences between legal systems merely concern legal form and technique but not differing values and preferences, harmonisation might be achieved at relatively low costs. Nonetheless, it remains a matter of empirical evidence whether the harmonisation costs would indeed be so low, even in areas where preferences do not differ that much.

Take the example of the negligence regime. Although the economic issue that the judge has to deal with in negligence cases is probably pretty similar all over Europe (examining whether the behaviour of the defendant comes up to a required standard of due care), there seem to be huge differences in the legal techniques used to arrive at the result[70]. One may, from an economic (some would argue naive) perspective, argue that, since the task of the judge in all of these negligence cases is always rather similar, it should be possible to lay down common rules on how the judge should set a standard of due care and weigh the behaviour of the defendant in all of these negligence cases, thereby doing away with all the different legal techniques used in the Member States[71]. One might then argue that the benefits would be that it would be a lot easier for legal practitioners to, for example, practise in other countries[72]. However, it would be rather naive to assume that all these differences merely constitute technicalities (though this may be true from an economic perspective). Given the fact that they are so heavily rooted in the legal system, the costs of harmonisation may again be huge. Some have already pointed out these difficulties in the literature.

However, here again "the proof of the pudding is in the eating". If it were possible at relatively low costs to harmonise, for example, the cases where strict liability is appropriate or the application of the negligence standard, this might be considered a benefit. However, harmonisation attempts so far (which we will discuss below) do not give cause for great optimism in this respect[73].

---

70 On these differences, see inter alia Helmut KOZIOL (ed), Unification of Tort Law: Wrongfulness, The Hague-London-New York 1998.

71 On all of these differing legal techniques, see Christian VON BAR, The Common European Law of Torts, vol II, Oxford 2000, 201–332.

72 Again, it ought to be pointed out that these benefits should not be overstated, since other legal rules may restrict their freedom to practise their profession in other countries.

73 See, however, the first results of the harmonisation attempt by the Study Group on a European Civil Code, presented by Christian VON BAR, Konturen des Deliksrechtskonzeptes der Study Group on a European Civil Code, (2001) ZEuP 515–532.

Moreover, one should always be careful that the transaction cost reduction argument does not disregard differences in preferences. In other words, if the current differences between the tort rules of various legal systems do indeed merely consist of technical differences and do not reflect differing preferences of citizens, the transaction cost reduction argument may be valid. One would then still have to be careful that in the area of negligence, for example, only the way that due care standards are set and how the judge weighs the behaviour of the injurer are harmonised, not, for example, the contents of the due care standard itself. What is required of an injurer, for instance a physician in a medical malpractice case, may well be different in Portugal from what it is in Sweden. Again, it cannot be argued here that these differences are merely pointless incompatibilities: they can actually be linked to differing preferences. Hence, the transaction cost reduction argument may lead to centralisation, but not necessarily to harmonisation[74]. This would mean that if it were possible at all at a relatively low cost to, for example, define how judges should deal with the negligence standard, that issue could be centralised, but the specific contents of the due care standard could still be left to national judges. This shows that, as has often been mentioned in the economic literature also, centralisation should not necessarily lead to complete harmonisation. Centralisation of the negligence standard in this example may well be combined with differences in the specific contents of this standard, by continuing to rely on national judges. Thus one could gain by lowering transaction costs (assuming that this were possible) and still have the benefit of respecting differing preferences.

There are, moreover, probably areas in private law where the differing preferences are much more significant than the reduction of transaction cost benefits. Take the example of the amounts awarded for non-pecuniary losses. Many have argued that there are still considerable differences between the Member States in that respect. However, it is relatively difficult to argue that these differences themselves lead to huge economic problems. Again, one could argue that these differences reflect differing national preferences and hence, there seems to be no point in favour of harmonisation there. In this case, the differences are probably not just differences in legal technique and can therefore not be reduced to pointless incompatibilities. It is, therefore, difficult to see any transaction cost benefit from harmonisation there, whereas the disadvantages (in terms of not respecting national preferences)

[74] Alessandra ARCURI, Controlling Environmental Risk in Europe: the complementary Role of an EC Environmental Liability Regime, (2001) Tijdschrift voor Milieuaansprakelijkheid (TMA) 41–42.

under harmonisation would be huge. From an economic perspective, there would, hence, be no argument for harmonisation of, say, the specific amounts awarded in the various cases of non-pecuniary losses[75].

But again, it should be stressed that the transaction cost reduction argument is in any case much more powerful than the argument for the harmonisation of marketing conditions, which has been used by Europe so far to justify its harmonisation efforts in the area of private law. However, it remains an empirical question whether the transaction costs corresponding to the current differences between the legal systems are indeed higher than the transaction costs of harmonisation.

*b) Example: product liability*

The transaction costs argument may play an important role in justifying the coordination of product safety standards to prevent states from hindering the free flow of products and services[76]. Indeed, some co-operation between states seems necessary if a product is mass-produced and internationally distributed, in order to avoid interstate trade being hampered as a result of varying national product safety standards[77]. Indeed, in international trade law too it is well-known that divergent health, safety and related regulatory standards between countries of origin and countries of destination, especially in cases where these standards are more stringent in the countries of destination, provoke allegations by the countries of origin that they are subject to discrimination in the countries of destination. This might result in a violation of GATT regulations and regulatory harmonisation will therefore ensue in order to minimise product incompatibilities so that producers have maximum access to export markets. Harmonisation is therefore certainly useful to avoid pointless incompatibilities which do not reflect different preferences[78]. These transaction costs arguments do therefore apply in the field of economic regulation and product safety. Indeed, the information required to formulate these rules may be useful for the whole of Europe and the formulation of uniform rules in these cases may save on information costs and can, hence, promote interstate trade. Therefore, once more, the Directive on General Product Safety, seen in the framework of the 1992 programme to

---

75 We return to the harmonisation of non-pecuniary losses in this paragraph under 5.

76 See generally David VOGEL (supra fn 39) 52–55.

77 Gary SCHWARTZ, Considering the Proper Federal Role in American Tort Law, (1996) 38 Arizona Law Review (ALR) 924–925.

78 Michael TREBILCOCK/Robert HOWSE, Trade Liberalization and Regulatory Diversity, Reconciling Competitive Markets with Competitive Politics, (1999) 6 European Journal of Law and Economics (EJLE) 21 and 30.

establish the internal market, may well be considered to be an instrument which saves on transaction costs[79].

The question, however, arises as to whether these transaction cost savings as a result of harmonised rules can also be expected for product liability. One could argue that a manufacturer who markets his products across the whole of Europe would, in the absence of harmonisation, need specialised legal counsel in every state and that his insurance underwriters would have to calculate the liability exposure separately in accordance with each state's product liability law[80]. This argument, however, as mentioned above, neglects the fact that there is a benefit in differentiated liability rules that reflect varying preferences. Moreover, the cost of harmonisation in the field of private law (which is so rooted in legal culture) may be huge and the alleged transaction cost savings may be less than expected. Indeed, even in the case of a harmonised legal rule, manufacturers would still need local counsels to bring their case to court. Accordingly, economies of scale under a harmonised rule would probably be insignificant[81]. Here again "the proof of the pudding is in the eating", so that the question arises of whether the European Product Liability Directive has been able to create the legal certainty required, reducing transaction costs for manufacturers[82].

Above, we looked more closely at the Product Liability Directive and argued that, given its dependence on national law, it can never lead to a harmonisation of marketing conditions. The Product Liability Directive in fact adds an additional layer of complexity to the labyrinth of conflicting standards of liability. It can therefore never lead to uniformity or a lowering of transaction costs[83].

---

79 Roger VAN DEN BERGH, (1998) MJ 145–146.

80 Robert ACKERMAN, Tort Law and Federalism: Whatever Happened to Devolution?, (1996) Yale Law and Policy Review (YLPR) 453.

81 Thus, ROBERT ACKERMAN, (1996) YLPR 453, note 135. See similarly for the European Product Liability Directive Michael FAURE, Productaansprakelijkheid in België en Europa: quo vadis?, in: Eric DIRIX et al. (eds.), Liber Amicorum Jacques Herbots, Deurne 2002, 111–130.

82 Van den Bergh rightly points to lots of interpretation problems in the European Product Liability Directive which supports the conclusion that the transaction cost savings may be small, simply because a full harmonisation of the rules of private law is apparently difficult to achieve (Roger VAN DEN BERGH, (1998) MJ 146–147).

83 See Robert ACKERMAN, (1996) YLPR 454.

## 5. Minimum level of protection

*a) General*

We will now leave the economic criteria for harmonisation and address whether other, non-economic arguments can be advanced in favour of the harmonisation of private law. This is a difficult and slippery road and therefore I want to remain brief here. Some may indeed argue that it is not economic arguments that demand the harmonisation of private law in Europe but, for example, the desire to provide a minimum level of protection to accident victims in the whole of Europe. Indeed, one also has the impression that a movement such as that in favour of a European civil code is more inspired by political idealism than by economic arguments. Nevertheless, some comment is possible on the idea that there should be a harmonisation of private law to guarantee a minimum level of protection to the citizens of Europe, more particularly to accident victims.

On paper this idea of guaranteeing a minimum quality to European citizens sounds nice. However, one should also realise that, as will be argued below, a minimum level of protection might be imposed upon citizens, even if this would not correspond with their preferences. Economists may argue that this amounts to paternalism. Moreover, economists have also argued against this idea of harmonisation on the basis of providing a minimum quality, since European policy so far has never aimed at providing a basic quality of life for all European citizens. If that were a political desire it would of course be far more important to provide, for example, minimum social security, basic health care and harmonisation in the area of minimum wages. Those areas are traditionally still very sensitive and related to national sovereignty and Europe has not intervened in them yet. It would therefore be rather strange to legislate towards a European civil code on the ground that European citizens should receive adequate protection when such minimum protection is not provided for more basic needs.

Moreover, it is questionable whether private law itself is an appropriate instrument to provide this minimum level of protection. The human rights arguments for harmonisation may be quite valid, but it is hard to see how these could be applied to the area of private law[84]. Moreover, one may argue that other instruments, based on the European Convention on Human Rights, would be more appropriate to provide this minimum level than the top-down harmonisation approach followed by the European Union.

---

[84] Unless the principle of equality is used as a justification for the harmonisation of tort law. See Jaap Spier/Olav O. Haazen, (1999) ZEuP 479–480.

Finally, it is also questionable whether the differences in private law levels today are serious enough to allow one to argue that in some Member States the minimum level of protection that a state should guarantee to its accident victims has not been provided. In sum, even the political argument in favour of a (total) harmonisation of private law (or even in favour of a minimum level) is rather weak.

*b) Example: non-pecuniary losses*

In the framework of a comparison of amounts awarded for non-pecuniary losses in Europe, it was indeed established that serious differences still exist, not only with respect to the question of whether some victims (and their relatives) are entitled to compensation for non-pecuniary losses, but also as far as the amounts awarded are concerned[85]. Some have therefore argued that it is unacceptable that within Europe a victim who, for example, suffers the loss of an arm would receive less, say in, Portugal than in Germany. They implicitly argue that there is no reason to treat those victims differently and that the call for harmonisation of the amounts awarded for non-pecuniary losses is justified[86].

What can, again, be said about this argument from an economic perspective? *First* of all one should remember that the differences in amounts awarded for non-pecuniary losses are certainly not pointless, but may reflect the differing preferences of the citizens in the various states. In this respect one should, *second*, also remember that Coase taught that every increase in protection can always be passed on via the price mechanism[87]. In other words if, for example, in the area of product liability, one argued that the Portuguese should award higher amounts for non-pecuniary losses to victims of product accidents, this would lead to an increase in prices. Indeed, the manufacturer will add the additional damage costs to the price of the products. The effect

[85] For an overview of the current differences between the Member States as far as the amounts awarded for pain and suffering are concerned see Horton W.V. ROGERS (ed), Damages for Non-Pecuniary Loss in a Comparative Perspective, Vienna-New York 2001.

[86] This argument is made by Ulrich MAGNUS/Jörg FEDTKE, German Report on non-pecuniary loss, in: Horton W.V. ROGERS (ed), Damages for non-pecuniary loss in a Comparative Perspective, Vienna-New York 2001, 109–128, and in Ulrich MAGNUS, Towards European Civil Liability, in: Michael FAURE/Hildegard SCHNEIDER/Jan SMITS (eds), Towards a European Ius Commune in legal education and research, Antwerpen-Groningen 2002; also compare Ulrich MAGNUS, European Perspectives on Tort Liability, (1995) European Review of Private Law (ERPL) 427–444.

[87] Ronald COASE, The problem of social cost, (1960) JLE 1–44.

therefore is that consumers pay a higher price for the protection awarded. It may well be that consumers in Portugal are not willing to pay this higher price. A European intervention forcing all Europeans to come up to, say, the German level, would therefore amount to paternalism.

*Third*, there may well be specific reasons why certain countries award relatively low amounts for non-pecuniary losses and others higher. To some extent this may be related to the level of social security. It is difficult to judge, but with respect to the difference between the US system and the European system, some claim that the high awards for non-pecuniary losses in the US constitute to some extent compensation for the fact that there is no general basic social security system in the US. Moreover, no one would claim that the European awards for non-pecuniary losses should come up to the American level.

Some argue that given the greater amount of travel in Europe today (tourism), it cannot be understood why, say, a German professor would receive less for his pain and suffering if he were to have an accident in Portugal rather than in Germany[88]. Again, this is hardly an argument in favour of harmonisation. Indeed, the fact that the Portuguese choose a lower level of compensation for pain and suffering than the Germans reflects differing preferences. There is no reason why the Portuguese should – paternalistically – have to come up to the German level, just to please the German tourist. The latter can, moreover, in the awareness that he will not enjoy the same level of protection abroad as in Germany, seek additional protection – if he so desires – in the form of a voluntary first party insurance. Such insurance for tourists is widely available on the market. The mere fact of tourism can, therefore, hardly be considered an argument in favour of harmonisation.

In sum, contrary to what is sometimes assumed, there may be very clear reasons why some countries have lower or higher levels of compensation for non-pecuniary losses than others. If this corresponds with differing preferences, one can, at least from an economic perspective, see no need for a general harmonisation merely because the existence of such differences is "unjust"[89].

---

[88] See – again – Ulrich MAGNUS/Jörg FEDTKE (supra fn 86).

[89] For a similar analysis, see Ton HARTLIEF, comments on Magnus, U., "Towards European Civil Liability", in: Michael FAURE/Hildegard SCHNEIDER/Jan SMITS (eds), Towards a European Ius Commune in legal education and research, Antwerpen-Groningen 2002.

## *IV. Policy aspects*

### 1. General

The result of applying economic criteria to the question of whether private law should be harmonised is that there would only be arguments in favour of centralised European rule making (1) if inefficiencies were fostered by national private law so that damage could be externalised to other countries or (2) if it could be established that states would attract industry by their lenient private law standards. The latter is, however, unlikely since states would, on the contrary, be more likely to enact legislation with high standards to protect accident victims within their own jurisdiction. However, there may be transaction cost savings if European intervention were able to create legal certainty and achieve full harmonisation. Other arguments, such as the need to create a "level playing field" or "the harmonisation of marketing conditions" cannot, at least from an economic perspective, justify centralisation.

Looking more specifically at the Product Liability Directive and comparing this to the criteria for centralisation we can conclude as follows:

1. The EC Product Liability Directive is not able to counteract the risk of interstate externalities caused by product damage, if such a risk already exists.
2. There is no empirical evidence of a risk that states could attract manufacturers with lenient product liability legislation (the directive would only apply to manufacturers). On the contrary, there might be a risk of a race for the top, protecting national victims of product-related accidents.
3. The Product Liability Directive, given its high reliance on national law, can never lead to a "levelling of the playing field" or a "harmonisation of marketing conditions".
4. The Product Liability Directive, which in fact adds an additional layer of complexity to the labyrinth of conflicting standards of liability, does not lead to uniformity or a lowering of transaction costs[90].

### 2. Public choice considerations

A question which obviously cannot be avoided when inefficiencies are found is whether this can be explained on the basis of public choice theory. Indeed, one notices that many of the harmonisation efforts do not fit into the economic theory of centralisation and would hence, at least from an economic

[90] Compare Robert ACKERMAN, (1996) YLPR 454.

perspective, not be considered to promote social welfare. If a certain legislative action cannot be said to promote the public interest, public choice scholars would ask whether the legislation favours special interest groups[91]. Of course, one can generally hold that the lack of transparency at the European level is a highly useful cover for lobbying activities. Below are two examples which may prove that the desire to create a European liability regime sometimes simply serves the interests of industry and is the result of lobbying.

Some have argued that the comparative lawyers themselves can be considered a lobby group. Harmonisation efforts will undoubtedly serve their interests since harmonisation requires knowledge of the various legal systems that need to be harmonised. A call for harmonisation does undoubtedly create a demand for comparative lawyers and may hence serve their interests[92].

Finally, in the context of public choice analysis, one should obviously also mention the interests of European bureaucracy itself. Until 1985 Europe had done relatively little as far as the harmonisation of private law was concerned (because differing legal cultures hampered it). Perhaps the European Product Liability Directive, although it did not fulfil the economic criteria for centralisation, may have served the interests of the Brussels bureaucracy by showing that Europe could bring about a piece of legislation in an area which is considered important by many lawyers, touches upon manufacturers' interests and is moreover very sensitive to public opinion. Hence, the fact that the Commission wanted a European Product Liability Directive may to some extent also simply have been because of the prestige that this directive, as one of the first in the area of private law, would give the European Commission.

### 3. Example: environmental liability

We concluded that relatively few economic arguments can be found to justify centralisation in the area of environmental liability. Only transboundary pollution justified it and even then the question arose as to whether the same result could not be reached through different legal instruments less extensive than total harmonisation.

---

[91] For a discussion of harmonisation efforts in Europe from a public choice perspective, see Roger Van den Bergh, (1998) MJ 148–151 and Roger Van den Bergh, (2000) 53 Kyklos 448–451, and see the recent paper by Richard Revesz, Federalism and Environmental Regulation: a public choice analysis, (2001) HLR 553–641.

[92] Thus, Anthony Ogus, (1999) ICLQ 405, and Anthony Ogus (supra fn 8) 28–32, as well as Roger Van den Bergh, (2000) 53 Kyklos 449.

Nevertheless, we found that there seem to be strong forces in Brussels striving for a European environmental liability regime, at least for damage to biodiversity. This resulted in a recent directive in this domain.[93] To some extent this can still be explained on public interest grounds, since we also indicated that non-economic, ecological arguments could be advanced, in favour of a minimum quality of reclamation for polluted soils. However, public choice scholars have taught that there is always a risk that regulation in fact serves the interests of particular pressure groups[94].

Indeed, another non-economic reason why the European Union would like to harmonise liability legislation can be found in public choice theory. With respect to environmental standard-setting, intensive rent-seeking behaviour by interest groups can be identified. European industries may be confronted at state level by "green" non-governmental organisations (NGOs), whereas these countervailing powers might have less force in Brussels. Moreover, the lack of transparency in the decision-making process, which is often used to reproach the European Union, will stimulate European industries to engage in serious lobbying.

The lobbying does not necessarily have to result in lower environmental standards. In particular cases, special interest groups representing industry might, understandably, lobby in favour of harmonisation at a higher level of environmental protection[95]. Interest groups in areas that are already heavily regulated may have incentives to extend their strict (national) regulations to the European level, forcing foreign competitors to follow the same strict regulation with which they already comply. The result is, again, that industry will lobby to erect artificial barriers to entry. In addition, green NGOs will be pleased with this lobby and will obviously support the demand to transfer strict national standards into a European standard[96]. Thus, industry in heavily regulated (and probably polluted) areas can (supported by green NGOs) force their very stringent standards upon their (southern) competi-

[93] See Directive 2004/35/EC of 21 April 2004 on environmental liability with regard to prevention and remedying of environmental damage. For a comment see the contributions in Gerrit BETLEM/Edward BRANS (eds), Environmental liability in the EU. The 2004 Directive compared with US and Member State law, London 2006.

[94] For a public choice analysis of (de)centralisation of environmental law see John FEREJOHN, The political economy pollution control in a federal system, in: Richard REVESZ/Philippe SANDS/Richard STEWART, Environmental Law, the Economy and Sustainable Development, Cambridge 2000, 96–103.

[95] See also Dan ESTY/Damien GERADIN, (1997) 21 HELR 303.

[96] These "alliances" between environmentalists and domestic producers are also discussed in David VOGEL (supra fn 39) 52–55.

tors, although these Member States probably would not need these stringent standards if the policy goal were only that of reaching a uniform level of environmental quality.

Thus, it becomes clear that the "harmonisation of conditions of competition" argument is used to serve the interests of industries in heavily regulated areas by erecting barriers to entry. Hence, environmental law can be used to limit market entry and environmental law is abused to serve private interest goals.

This leads to the conclusion that the "harmonisation of conditions of competition" argument, as presented in European rhetoric, can be problematic, from both the economic and ecological points of view, and in fact serves the interests of industrial groups in heavily regulated areas[97]. It can actually be in their interests that "conditions of competition" are harmonised.

It is not clear yet whether the recent harmonization efforts with respect to environmental liability should be considered an attempt by interest groups to create barriers to entry. One could still run the risk that industry in Member States with stringent soil reclamation regulations would strive for centralisation, thus creating a barrier to entry for competitors from countries where these strict standards do not yet apply. It is too early to assess whether the desire to create a European environmental liability regime in fact serves the interest of industry. One should, however, always be aware of the fact that this risk, that centralisation may be abused to create barriers to entry, may always appear in any attempt towards centralisation.

## *V. Concluding remarks*

Today there is undoubtedly a general trend among academic lawyers in favour of the harmonisation of private law in Europe[98]. Symptomatic in this respect are major projects such as those focusing on a European civil code. In this paper, I did not focus on the complicated question of how such a harmonisation of private law in Europe could be achieved, nor did I focus on the actual differences between the private laws of the European Member States

---

[97] This is not to say that there is no risk of regulatory capture resulting in inefficient standards at the level of the Member States, compare (in the US context) Susan ROSE-ACKERMAN (supra fn 4) 166 and 173. However, in Europe, it is especially the untransparent Brussels bureaucracy which is feared from a public choice perspective.

[98] See eg Nils JANSEN, Auf dem Weg zu einem europäischen Haftungsrecht, (2001) ZEuP 30–65. Helmut KOZIOL, (1996) ZEuP 587–599 and Ulrich MAGNUS, (1995) ERPL 427–444 and compare Johannes H. NIEUWENHUIS, Wat is een onrechtmatige daad? Europese perspectieven, (1998) RMThemis 242–248.

today. This paper used the economic analysis of law to focus on one specific aspect of the harmonisation debate, the question of whether there should be any harmonisation at all and if so, in what areas. One indeed sometimes gets the impression that this basic question concerning the need for harmonisation seems to be forgotten as a result of a great enthusiasm for the challenge of harmonisation. In this paper, I have tried to show that the economic analysis of law, more specifically the economics of federalism, provides balanced answers to questions about harmonisation.

The starting point for economic analysis is seemingly different from the one often heard in the European debate[99]. Economists stress that differences as such are not a bad thing at all, provided that those differences also reflect the differing preferences of citizens[100]. If that is the case, the starting point is that these differences should be respected and that they may even contribute to an increased quality of the legal system because legal systems will compete to provide the best legal order to their citizens. Of course, some may argue that it is questionable whether the fact that in Portugal, say, lower amounts are awarded for pain and suffering than in Germany, really reflects the preferences of the Portuguese citizens. That is, however, a dangerous line of reasoning. It questions the ability of a national legislator or judge to set damage awards according to the preferences of the citizens and therefore basically questions the democratic nature of the decision-making process in that respect. Moreover, even if one does doubt the ability of the national legislator or judge to adequately take into account the preferences of citizens, there is still no reason to assume that Europe would do a better job in that respect. Why should we assume that the European bureaucrats in Brussels would be more likely to know what the preferences of the Portuguese are than the Portuguese would be to find this out for themselves? This is a paternalistic and dangerous argument. Legislation that allows for different

---

[99] See also Claus OTT/Hans-Bernd SCHÄFER, Die Vereinheitlichung des Europäischen Vertragsrechts. Ökonomische Notwendigkeit oder akademisches Interesse?, in: Claus OTT/Hans-Bernd SCHÄFER (eds), Vereinheitlichung und Diversität des Zivilrechts in transnationalen Wirtschaftsräumen, Tübingen 2003, 203–236 and Jan SMITS, On successful legal transplants in a future Ius Commune Europaeum, in: Andrew HARDING/Esin ÖRÜCÜ (eds), Comparative law in the 21st century, London The Hague New York 2002, 137–15; Jan SMITS, Toward a multi-layered contract law for Europe, in Stefan GRUNDMAN/Jules STUYCK (eds), An academic green paper on European contract law, The Hague 2002, 387–398 and Jan SMITS, The harmonisation of private law in Europe: some insights from evolutionary theory, (2002) 31 Georgia Journal of International and Comparative Law 79–99.

[100] Some lawyers also follow this line of reasoning. See eg Jan SMITS, The good Samaritan in European private law, Mechelen 2000, 43, who presents "In praise of Diversity".

national preferences will, moreover, have the advantage that it will lead to competition between legal orders.

However, it was equally indicated that in some cases this basic idea of competition between legal orders may not provide optimal outcomes. The economic literature makes clear that there may be an argument in favour of harmonisation where transboundary externalities exist, but this does not justify a total harmonisation of private law. It merely calls for a regulation of transboundary accidents at the centralised level. The other economic argument in favour of harmonisation is the risk of destructive competition, also referred to as the "race for the bottom". However, it seems very unlikely that within the European context, states will compete in order to attract industry with lenient private laws. There is no empirical evidence at all that current European Member States would engage in such a race for the bottom with an inefficient tort law. It is much more likely that a race for the top would take place, since states would probably prefer to protect those of their national citizens who might also suffer accidents.

Moreover, the traditional "economic" European argument – that harmonisation of the conditions of competition is necessary in order to create a level playing field – was critically discussed and rejected as wrong. This argument has been used for a long time in Europe. To some extent this was understandable, since the argument for the "harmonisation of marketing conditions" was necessary to give Europe competencies in specific matters. However, it is very doubtful whether such harmonisation of marketing conditions is desirable, since this could justify a (largely unnecessary) harmonisation of all sorts of legal rules, because all kinds of legislation could arguably have an influence on marketing conditions. Moreover, the initiatives that Europe has taken so far with respect to tort law have not proven to be a major success. All legal writers agree, for example, that the European Product Liability Directive could never lead to the harmonisation of marketing conditions. Moreover, the European directives generally seem to have the problem that they follow the "top-down" approach, whereby the European regime is mandatorily imposed upon the Member States, sometimes as an additional layer of protection, such as in the case of the European Product Liability Directive. This should lead to a critical review of the harmonisation efforts undertaken by the European Commission. Unfortunately, the Commission only seems interested in promoting further harmonisation instead of focusing on less (and maybe better) harmonisation[101].

---

101 See Green Paper on Liability for defective products (COM (1999) 396 final).

It is important to stress that from an economic perspective, probably the most important reason in favour of centralisation of tort law is the potential for reducing transaction costs. One can certainly argue to some extent that various tort rules in the Member States reflect similar preferences and only differ as a result of differing legal techniques and dogma. If it were possible to align rules of private law that reflect similar preferences, this could certainly be considered a gain. That is precisely the approach chosen in a variety of (mostly privately initiated) academic projects on harmonisation of private law[102]. In most of these projects the academics involved analyse the existing differences between the various aspects of private law in the Member States and try to find a common denominator. This approach seems to be more promising than that chosen by the European Commission. That top-down approach of imposing directives on Member States has so far not been very successful. The approach chosen by the academic groups focuses on the search for a *ius commune* and can therefore be called "bottom-up". If these groups succeed in showing that some differences are merely of a technical nature and can thus be considered pointless incompatibilities which do not touch upon or relate to differing preferences, then this harmonisation approach of searching for a common denominator may well prove to be more successful than the approach chosen by the European Commission so far.

Moreover, the work of these groups has the advantage that their proposals for a European private law are based on a general concept of private law. The various approaches chosen so far in the European directives are so different that it is clear that any general concept is totally lacking[103].

Whether these groups will be successful is obviously difficult to predict. Some have stressed the importance of legal tradition and legal principles.

---

[102] It is not possible to mention all the harmonization projects with respect to private law here (for an overview of all the projects, see Ewoud H. HONDIUS, Towards a European civil code?, paper presented at the Lustrum Conference, at Maastricht on 25–26 October 2001 and Nils JANSEN, (2001) ZEuP 31–65). For the area of tort law, we can refer to the Principles project of the European Group on tort law, supervised by Helmut KOZIOL (Vienna). For an overview of their method and work, see Jaap SPIER/Olav HAAZEN, (1999) ZEuP 469–493. In 2005 their principles were published. See EUROPEAN GROUP ON TORT LAW, Principles of European Tort Law, Vienna-New York 2006. Another initiative is part of the project on a European civil code, co-ordinated by Prof. VON BAR (Osnabrück). For an overview of their vision with respect to the harmonisation of tort law, see Christian VON BAR, (2000) ZEuP 515–532.

[103] Thus, Helmut KOZIOL, Ein europäisches Schadenersatzrecht – Wirklichkeit oder Traum, (2001) Juristische Blätter (JBl) 32–33 and Pierre WIDMER, Die Vereinheitlichung des europäischen Schadenersatzrechts aus der Sicht eines Kontinentaleuropäers, (1999) 52 Revue Hellénique de Droit International 99.

Indeed, from an economic perspective one can easily argue that different legal rules sometimes serve the same purpose and thus could easily be harmonised. However, in some cases these are so heavily rooted in differing legal cultures and traditions that the costs of harmonisation may be huge, some would argue even prohibitive[104]. From an economic perspective obviously, one can merely state that harmonisation based on potential for the reduction of transaction costs only makes sense if the marginal costs of this harmonisation effort are indeed lower than the marginal benefits of unification.

However, economics can provide few a guidelines to these unification groups as far as the topics and methods of harmonisation are concerned.

First, it seems important primarily to focus on those areas of private law where preferences apparently do not differ. One might think of the choice between a strict liability regime on the one hand and negligence/fault on the other hand. If it could be established that the legal systems largely agree on the area where a strict liability regime should be applied, then one could argue that the differences in form are merely technical and do not reflect varying preferences, so that that would be a good candidate for harmonisation[105].

The same could be argued, for example, with respect to the weighing of interests the judge has to undertake in a negligence case when he has to establish a standard of care for a particular behaviour and when the wrongfulness of the behaviour of the defendant has to be established. If the research groups found that, although the wordings and principles are dramatically different, the underlying methodology is similar, harmonisation might be possible[106]. However, the way in which a judge in a particular legal system

---

[104] That point has been made in particular by Pierre LEGRAND, (1997) MJ 111.

[105] I certainly do not want to argue that there are no differences between the Member States as far as the cases are concerned to which a strict liability rule applies. Some might argue that the differences, say, between France and the United Kingdom in that respect are huge (for an overview, see Bernhard A. KOCH/Helmut KOZIOL (ed) (supra fn 68) and see Walter VAN GERVEN/Jeremy LEVER/Pierre LAROUCHE (supra fn 69) 467–687 and see Christian VON BAR (supra fn 71) 333–432.). The point is merely that if there were – factual – agreement, say, on the strict liability of the guardian of a dangerous installation, this would mean that preferences on that point do not appear to differ.

[106] See on that point generally, Helmut KOZIOL (ed) (supra fn 70) and for a comparison of the wrongfulness concept in Austria and Germany, Helmut KOZIOL, (2001) JBl 29–38 and Peter LEWISCH, A comparison of the Negligence Concept of the German BGB and the Austrian ABGB in an Economic Perspective, paper presented at the Annual conference of the European Association of Law and Economics in Vienna, September 2001, as well as Cees VAN DAM, Aansprakelijkheidsrecht. Een grensoverschrijdend handboek, The Hague 2000, 143–150.

will fulfil this duty of care may again be strongly linked to differing preferences. Thus, specifically, it would be possible to indicate that whatever the methods judges use to establish negligence in a particular case, it may still be possible that in a medical malpractice case, for example, the appropriate care required of a physician in Portugal may well be different from the care required of a physician in Germany[107]. This shows that it may be possible to call for centralisation, but that this centralisation should not necessarily be equated with harmonisation[108]. The previous example shows that it would, for example, be possible to centralise the way judges deal with the negligence standard, but this could be combined with a differentiated application of the duty of care in specific cases[109]. Thus one could use a *flexible system*[110] with a harmonisation of some general notions at the European level, but on the other hand retention of a sufficient degree of flexibility to account for the diverging preferences of Member States.

The example, again, shows that harmonisation cannot be addressed in black and white statements. Some issues may be harmonised at relatively low cost, whereas others (which are closely related to preferences) can be differentiated. To provide another example and guideline: one should probably be very careful when striving for harmonisation in those areas of private law which are indeed clearly linked to national preferences and values. This is probably the case for the issue of compensation for non-pecuniary losses. Here one should be very careful in calling for harmonisation[111]. First of all, the benefits of harmonisation in that area should be made clear; second, it is very likely that the costs of harmonisation would be huge and; third, harmonisation in those cases could lead to a paternalistic measure and to disrespect

---

107 Comparative research has indicated that this is indeed the case. See Michael FAURE/Helmut KOZIOL (eds), Cases on Medical Malpractice in a Comparative Perspective, Vienna-New York 2001.

108 This was correctly argued in the context of environmental liability by Alessandra ARCURI, (2001) TMA.

109 See, however, Helmut KOZIOL, (2001) JBl 33, who argues that a harmonization effort with mere vague notions whereby the normative choices in specific cases would still be left to the national legislators or judges would not suffice. Jaap SPIER/Olav HAAZEN, (1999) ZEuP 484) also see this problem where they argue "the use of standards as a smoke-screen for deep disagreement creates a false consensus".

110 This idea of a flexible system in tort law comes from the Austrian scholar Walter WILBURG, Die Elemente des Schadenersatzrechts, Marburg an der Lahn 1941, and the same, Entwicklung eines beweglichen Systems im bürgerlichen Recht, Graz 1950. See also Helmut KOZIOL, Rechtswidrigkeit, bewegliches System und Rechtsausgleichung, (1988) JBl 619.

111 See also Ton HARTLIEF (supra fn 89).

for the preferences of citizens. Even a call to the need to provide the same minimum protection to all accident victims within Europe can hardly justify such a paternalistic measure.

However, with this statement and the reference to the need for providing a basic level of victim protection we have left the area of economics. Indeed, the reader should recall once more that in this paper, I have only provided "one view of the cathedral". I have merely addressed the question of whether a harmonisation of private law is needed from an economic perspective. This is not totally useless, since the European Commission itself has long advanced an economic ground (harmonisation of marketing conditions) to justify European action. That reason is, as I have tried to show in this paper, particularly weak.

The conclusion at the normative level, however, should not necessarily be that there is no need for any European action at all with respect to private law[112]. My main problem is that the Commission still seems to be stuck in the old jargon of the "harmonisation of conditions of competition", whereas that seems to be a weak reason for harmonisation. There may be other, non-economic, reasons to justify harmonisation. But then these goals and expectations should be spelled out more specifically. Even those who dream of a European tort law as a political ideal (and who should realise that this may violate the preferences of citizens) can still benefit from economic analysis. Economics can help to show whether the methods of harmonisation chosen in a particular case can lead to the goals advertised. Moreover, those who blindly follow an unbalanced harmonisation dream should also be aware of the fact that in some cases they may (probably unknowingly) be instruments in the hands of powerful lobby groups who can benefit from harmonisation. In this respect, the important lesson from the public choice school, that whenever inefficient regulatory measures are enacted there is usually a special interest group that benefits from this action, should not be forgotten.

Moreover, it seems important to take the subsidiarity principle seriously in the debate on the harmonisation of tort law within Europe. Within the context of that debate, attention should obviously also be given to the legal

---

[112] Compare Jaap SPIER/Olav HAAZEN, (1999) ZEuP 477: "Nor is convergence or unification of private law ever strictly speaking necessary… If we favour convergence of European private law, we deem it simply desirable, perhaps highly desirable, but nothing more". This desirability of the harmonisation of private law in Europe is, however, highly criticised – inter alia – by Jan M. SMITS, Waarom harmonisering van het contractenrecht (via beginselen) onwenselijk is, (2001) Contracteren 73–74.

basis for justification efforts in the area of private law. If these European legal issues are addressed more carefully (which was not the topic of this paper) the conclusion may be reached that, given the subsidiarity principle, a general harmonisation effort concerning private law is problematic and that a balanced approach, focusing on (a modest) harmonisation in specific areas, may be more warranted. Then the economic criteria which can provide a balanced approach to the harmonisation issue would again be helpful.

# Rechtsvereinheitlichung auf europäischer Ebene aus privatrechtlicher Sicht

HELMUT KOZIOL*

## *Einleitung*

Bei Salzburg kommt es unmittelbar an der Grenze zu Deutschland zu einem Verkehrsunfall, in den eine Belgierin und ein Deutscher mit ihren Kraftfahrzeugen verwickelt sind; beide werden verletzt und die beiden mitfahrenden Ehegatten getötet. Ich möchte auf die hier doch nebensächlichen Sachschäden nicht eingehen, sondern nur auf die Personenschäden.

Für Schadenersatzansprüche ist die Rechtsordnung des Staates maßgebend, in dessen Hoheitsgebiet sich der Unfall ereignete[1]; nicht die Heimatrechtsordnung der Beteiligten. In unserem Beispiel könnte nun unter Umständen strittig sein, auf welcher Seite der Grenzlinie die Kollision erfolgte und es wäre für den Juristen besonders unangenehm, wenn der Zusammenprall genau auf der Grenzlinie geschah: Die Rechtsordnungen beider Länder können ja nicht zugleich anwendbar sein.

Sehen wir aber von diesem unlösbaren Fall ab: Weshalb ist es überhaupt relevant, ob deutsches oder österreichisches Recht anwendbar ist? Nun, die anwendbare Rechtsordnung ist für Inhalt und Umfang der zustehenden Ersatzansprüche bedeutsam. Es gibt nämlich nicht nur Unterschiede bezüglich der Ersatz-Höchstbeträge, sondern auch bei der Frage, welche Schäden auszugleichen sind: Die nach den nationalen Rechtsordnungen zustehenden Ansprüche auf Ersatz der durch die Körperverletzung oder Tötung entstehenden Vermögensschäden, wie Heilungskosten, Verdienstentgang und sonstige Folgekosten, aber auch und in noch stärkerem Ausmaß die Ansprüche auf Ausgleich der dem Verletzten oder den Hinterbliebenen entstandenen

---

* Direktor der Forschungsstelle für Europäisches Schadenersatzrecht (ESR), Österreichische Akademie der Wissenschaften, Wien, Österreich.

[1] Art 3 des Haager Straßenverkehrsübereinkommens; das entspricht der allgemeinen Regel des § 48 Abs 1 IPRG.

ideellen Nachteile weisen gravierende Unterschiede auf[2]. In vielen europäischen Staaten (zB in Österreich, Belgien, Frankreich) steht Personen, die einen nahen Angehörigen bei einem Verkehrsunfall verloren haben, ein eigener Schmerzensgeldanspruch zu, der auf Ersatz des durch den Tod entstandenen Leides gerichtet ist; auf eine eigene Gesundheitsbeeinträchtigung (zB Schock durch die Todesnachricht) kommt es dabei nicht an. In mehreren anderen Mitgliedstaaten der EU (zB Deutschland oder die Niederlande) wird hingegen ein solches Angehörigenschmerzensgeld nicht zuerkannt. Das kann je nach dem, ob die Unfallstelle einen Meter vor oder nach der Grenze liegt, zu ganz unterschiedlichen Schmerzensgeldbeträgen für die eigene Verletzung führen, aber auch dazu, dass der Deutsche für den Verlust seiner Frau einen Ersatz bekommt, den er zu Hause nie erlangt hätte; oder umgekehrt, die Belgierin einen Ersatzanspruch nicht geltend machen kann, der ihr nach dem heimatlichen Recht selbstverständlich gebührte.

Bei einem Verkehrsunfall mit Auslandsberührung ist daher die Frage des anzuwendenden Rechts von entscheidender Bedeutung; die häufigen Meinungsverschiedenheiten über die international-privatrechtliche Anknüpfung verhindern häufig eine einvernehmliche Beilegung des Streitfalles und verursachen damit erhebliche Prozesskosten. Eine Harmonisierung des europäischen Haftungsrechts könnte daher zu einer spürbaren Verringerung der Rechtsstreitigkeiten und damit der Folgekosten eines Verkehrsunfalls führen; das gilt aber entsprechend für alle anderen Schadensfälle mit internationalem Bezug.

Durch die unterschiedlichen nationalen Regelungen über Art und Umfang des Schadensersatzes wird ferner auch der *grenzüberschreitende Handel* erheblich beeinträchtigt. Unternehmer, die ihre Waren oder Dienstleistungen in anderen Mitgliedsländern anbieten, werden gegenüber rein national agierenden Konkurrenten benachteiligt. Während sich nämlich die innerstaatlichen Anbieter ausschließlich über die rechtlichen Rahmenbedingungen ihrer Rechtsordnung informieren müssen, ist der ausländische Anbieter gezwungen, sich über eine von seinem Heimatrecht abweichende Rechtsordnung zu informieren und sich an diese zu halten. Hierdurch entstehen Transaktionskosten, die sich insbesondere für kleine und mittelständische Unternehmen als Marktzutrittsschranke erweisen können. Unterschiedlich strenge Haftungsregelungen können darüber hinaus nicht nur marktzugangsbeschränkende sondern zugleich wettbewerbsverfälschende Wirkung

---

[2] Siehe dazu ausführlich Bernhard A. KOCH/Helmut KOZIOL (Hrsg), Compensation for Personal Injury in a Comparative Perspective, Wien-New York 2003; das Werk enthält auch eine vergleichende Analyse in deutscher Sprache.

haben, da die Haftungsbedingungen im Herkunftsland die Kostenkalkulation beeinflussen.

Wirtschaftsfernere Bereiche – beispielsweise die Haftung der Eltern für ihre Kinder, der Tierhalter oder der Grundstückseigentümer – führen dagegen zwar nicht zu direkten Wettbewerbsverzerrrungen. Dennoch weisen auch diese Materien mittelbar über das *Haftpflichtversicherungswesen* Bezüge zum Binnenmarkt auf.

Bedenkt man die eben dargestellten Schwierigkeiten, die mit der Lösung der Frage verbunden sind, welche Rechtsordnung in internationalen Schadensfällen anzuwenden ist, so liegt es sicherlich nicht fern, von einem einheitlichen Recht zu träumen, das all diese Anknüpfungsprobleme überflüssig macht. Das ist derzeit sicherlich noch ein Traum, der aber doch wenigstens teilweise realisierbar erscheint, insbesondere für das Vertragsrecht[3] sowie das Schadenersatzrecht[4] und beschränkt auf die Europäische Union. Wir werden später aber auch noch die Frage anschneiden müssen, ob es sich bei diesem Traum um einen Glückstraum oder einen Albtraum handelt.

## *Der unbefriedigende heutige Zustand*

Zunächst jedoch ein Blick auf den heutigen Zustand: In den letzten Jahrzehnten nahmen zwar die internationalen Bemühungen um eine Rechtsvereinheitlichung merkbar zu und sie haben auch zu bedeutsamen Ergebnissen geführt, allerdings nur für verhältnismäßig eng umgrenzte Gebiete. Es sei hier an das Wiener Kaufrechts-Übereinkommen erinnert.

Neben diesen weltweiten Bestrebungen ist derzeit vor allem in Europa eine vielfältige Rechtsvereinheitlichung oder zumindest Rechtsangleichung innerhalb der Europäischen Union festzustellen: Für viele Bereiche kommt es zu einer zentralen Rechtssetzung, insbesondere durch *Verordnungen* oder *Richtlinien*, die von den Mitgliedstaaten in nationales Recht umzusetzen sind und oft nicht bloß die Richtung der Regelung vorgeben, sondern dem nationalen Gesetzgeber nur sehr geringen Spielraum lassen. Diese Richtlinien haben im Gebiet des Zivilrechts vor allem in das Vertragsrecht, aber auch in

---

[3] Siehe insbesondere die Mitteilung der Kommission an den Rat und das Europäische Parlament zum Europäischen Vertragsrecht vom 11.7.2001, KOM (2001) 398 endg, Amtsblatt der Europäischen Union (ABl) Nr C 255 vom 13.09.2001, 1–44.

[4] Es liegen schon zwei Vorschläge für die künftige Ausgestaltung eines europäischen Schadenersatzrechtes vor, einer von der EUROPEAN GROUP ON TORT LAW, die mit der Forschungsstelle für Europäisches Schadenersatzrecht der Österreichischen Akademie der Wissenschaften zusammenarbeitet, und einer von der STUDY GROUP ON A EUROPEAN CIVIL CODE.

das Schadenersatzrecht eingewirkt. Ferner kommt der *Rechtsprechung* des Europäischen Gerichtshofs ein Vereinheitlichungseffekt zu. Darüber hinaus hat das *Europäische Parlament* schon mehrmals Vorbereitungsarbeiten für ein Europäisches Zivilgesetzbuch gefordert. Nach anfänglichem Widerstand sprachen sich nun auch die Regierungschefs der Mitgliedsländer für eine Rechtsannäherung aus und es scheint sich auch die Kommission für den Gedanken einer Vereinheitlichung des Vertragsrechtes etwas[5] zu erwärmen und sie unternimmt erste vorbereitende Schritte.

Anders als die politischen Instanzen beschäftigt sich die Wissenschaft schon seit Jahren eingehend mit der Schaffung eines einheitlichen europäischen Zivilgesetzbuches[6] oder mit der Vereinheitlichung größerer Teile des Privatrechts. Die Rechtsvereinheitlichung wird allerdings keineswegs einmütig gefordert oder auch nur als wünschenswert angesehen, vielmehr erheben sich warnende Stimmen, die sich gegen ein Gesetzbuch oder auch gegen die Vereinheitlichung wesentlicher Teile des Privatrechts aussprechen.[7]

Die *Ablehnung* kann sich ohne Zweifel auf einige gewichtige Gründe stützen: Die Rechtsordnung ist ein wesentliches Kulturgut jedes Staates, die sich in Jahrhunderten entwickelt hat, auf breiter Überzeugung beruht und das Zusammenleben prägt. Eine gesamteuropäische Kodifikation könnte daher zu einem einschneidenden Bruch mit der Tradition führen. Dieses Argument darf aber auch nicht überbewertet werden: Große Teile der heutigen europäischen Rechtsordnungen, wie insbesondere das Obligationenrecht, sind noch immer vom römischen Recht geprägt und weisen weitgehende Übereinstimmung auf; darauf hat vor allem *Reinhard Zimmermann* aufmerksam gemacht[8]. Im Schuldrecht käme es daher – wenn auch auf diese gemeinsamen Wurzeln Rücksicht genommen wird – nicht zu grundlegenden

---

5 Freilich scheint diese eher ein praktisches „Instrumentarium" („toolbox") bzw Handbuch für die Kommission und den EU-Gesetzgeber zur Verwendung bei der Überprüfung bestehender Rechtsvorschriften und der Erarbeitung neuer Rechtsvorschriften vorzusehen, vgl Kommission der Europäischen Gemeinschaften, Zweiter Fortschrittsbericht zum Gemeinsamen Referenzrahmen vom 25.7.2007, KOM (2007) 447 endg, 10.

6 Vgl etwa Peter-Christian MÜLLER-GRAFF, Zweiter Kodifikationsbeschluß des Europäischen Parlaments, Zeitschrift für Europäisches Privatrecht (ZEuP) 1995, 534; Jürgen BASEDOW, Europäisches Vertragsrecht für europäische Märkte, Bonn 1996; Arthur HARTKAMP/Martijn HESSELINK/Ewoud HONDIUS/Carla JOUSTRA/Edgar DU PERRON (eds), Towards a European Civil Code, 2nd ed The Hague-London-Boston 1998 mit weiteren Nachweisen.

7 Siehe etwa Pierre LEGRAND, Against a European Civil Code, Modern Law Review 1997, 44.

8 Reinhard ZIMMERMANN, The Law of Obligations, Roman Foundations of the Civilian Tradition, Oxford 1995.

Änderungen. Anderes gilt allerdings für Familien- und Erbrecht, sowie für Teile des Sachenrechts.

Mag auch ein europäisches Zivilgesetzbuch noch in weiter Ferne liegen, eine Auseinandersetzung mit der *Rechtsvereinheitlichung* an sich bleibt keinesfalls erspart: Die Rechtsvereinheitlichung innerhalb der Europäischen Union ist – wie schon erwähnt – eine nicht mehr zu leugnende Tatsache, mit der sich jeder Jurist abzufinden hat. Lediglich der Umfang und die Art der Durchführung stehen noch zur Diskussion.

Zieht man eine Bilanz der *bisherigen* Rechtsangleichung auf dem Gebiet des Privatrechts, so fällt diese leider recht *negativ* aus: Die Europäische Gemeinschaft hat seit ihrer Gründung eine erhebliche Zahl von Regelungen getroffen; eine umfassende Gesamtharmonisierung des europäischen Privatrechts wurde dagegen – wie schon erwähnt – bislang von ihr noch nicht in Angriff genommen. Die Richtlinien oder Verordnungen der EU betreffen vielmehr jeweils eng umgrenzte Bereiche. Diese *punktuelle Rechtsangleichung* führt zu einer *doppelten Rechtszersplitterung*: Es werden nicht nur die sehr unterschiedlichen nationalen Rechtsordnungen mit ihnen oft fremdartigen Regelungen durchsetzt[9], sondern auch die Richtlinien oder Verordnungen selbst beruhen *nicht* auf einem schlüssigen, konsequenten Gesamtkonzept, so dass sie widersprüchlich sind[10].

Das ist nun nicht etwas, worauf nur ein theoretisch interessierter Jurist stößt, sondern begegnet jedem von uns im täglichen Leben: Nehmen wir an, dass eine Salzburgerin einerseits ihrem Sohn in einem Salzburger Dorf von ihrem Konto bei einer Salzburger Bank einen Betrag auf dessen Konto bei der örtlichen Sparkasse überweist; nehmen wir anderseits an, die Salzburgerin überweist ihrer Tochter in Freilassing einen Betrag auf deren Bankkonto. Es dürfte die Annahme nahe liegen, dass eine Überweisung innerhalb Österreichs problemloser ist als eine nach Deutschland. Juristisch ist es aber nicht so: Die EU hat eine Richtlinie für grenzüberschreitende Überweisungen im EU-Raum erlassen und diese wurde im österreichischen Recht auch nur für solche Überweisungen umgesetzt[11]. Das führt dazu, dass die Überweisung

---

[9] Siehe dazu etwa Peter HOMMELHOFF, Zivilrecht unter dem Einfluss europäischer Rechtsangleichung, Archiv für die civilistische Praxis (AcP) 192 (1992) 102 ff; Ivo SCHWARTZ, Perspektiven der Angleichung des Privatrechts in der Europäischen Gemeinschaft, ZEuP 1994, 570; Helmut KOZIOL, Ein europäisches Schadenersatzrecht – Wirklichkeit und Traum, Juristische Blätter (JBl) 2001, 29 ff.

[10] Vgl hierzu Helmut KOZIOL, Die Vereinheitlichung des Europäischen Schadenersatzrechtes, in: Festschrift anlässlich des 75 Jahr-Jubiläums der Österreichischen Gesellschaft für Versicherungsfachwissen, Wien 2004, 56 f.

[11] Überweisungsgesetz, BGBl I 1999/123.

innerhalb von Salzburg weiterhin österreichischem Recht unterliegt; die Überweisung nach Deutschland hingegen dem neuen EU-geprägten Überweisungsgesetz. Läuft nun bei der Überweisung etwas schief, so trifft bei einer inländischen Überweisung das Risiko weitgehend die Überweisende. Bei der Auslandsüberweisung wird die Überweisende hingegen durch eine Garantie der Salzburger Bank gesichert. Man sieht aber auch wozu das führt: Bei einem so alltäglichen Massengeschäft wie einer Banküberweisung, sind auf ganz entsprechende Vorgänge völlig unterschiedliche Regelungen anzuwenden: Auf innerösterreichische Überweisungen österreichisches Recht; auf Überweisungen innerhalb der EU ist das Überweisungsgesetz für einen Teil der Fragen entscheidend; bei Überweisungen in das andere Ausland, sind nach internationalem Privatrecht in der Regel mehrere Rechtsordnungen heranzuziehen. Die Rechtsfolgen sind zum Teil ganz unterschiedlich, ohne dass es dafür eine sachliche Rechtfertigung gäbe und überdies passen die EU-Regelungen nicht in das österreichische Recht und erzeugen Wertungswidersprüche.

Weiteres Anschauungsmaterial, und zwar für das Schadenersatzrecht bietet insbesondere die Produkthaftungs-Richtlinie[12]: Es wird den Unternehmern eine strenge, verschuldensunabhängige Haftung für mangelhafte Produkte auferlegt. Es bleibt jedoch völlig offen, wie diese Haftung sich in ein Gesamtkonzept des Schadenersatzrechtes einfügt, das wohl ganz allgemein die Unternehmerhaftung erfassen müsste. Es fragt sich daher etwa, warum nicht auch Dienstleistungen erfasst sind und wie sich diese Haftung zu den in vielen Rechtsordnungen anerkannten Gefährdungshaftungen verhält.

Außer im Bereich der Normgebung wird das Fehlen eines Gesamtkonzepts auch in der Rechtsprechung des Gerichtshofs der Europäischen Gemeinschaften spürbar. Die *Staatshaftungsjudikatur* des Gerichtshofs hat zu schadenersatzrechtlich höchst bedeutsamen Entwicklungen geführt[13]: Die Mitgliedstaaten sind nun verpflichtet, die durch Gemeinschaftsrechtsverletzung herbeigeführten Schädigungen von Einzelpersonen auszugleichen. Dass die Mitgliedstaaten demnach auch für ein Fehlverhalten des Gesetzgebers einzustehen haben, ist für viele Rechtsordnungen eine bahnbrechende Neuerung. Bedenklich ist aber vor allem, dass im Bereich der auch sonst im Haftungsrecht relevanten Zurechnungsgründe Abweichungen von nahezu allen europäischen Rechtsordnungen festzustellen sind, die nicht ohne wei-

[12] ABl Nr L 210 vom 07.08.1985, 29 ff.

[13] Siehe dazu etwa Birgit Schoisswohl, Staatshaftung wegen Gemeinschaftsrechtsverletzung: Anspruchsgrundlage und materielle Voraussetzungen, Wien 2002.

teres einsichtig sind und zu Systembrüchen führen. Das gilt insbesondere für die Voraussetzung der qualifizierten Gemeinschaftsrechtsverletzung, die zum Teil als reines Erfolgsunrecht verstanden wird und daher schwerlich mit den meisten europäischen Haftungssystemen in Einklang zu bringen ist. Unbefriedigend ist auch die Wiedererweckung der Unmittelbarkeit des Kausalzusammenhanges durch den EuGH, die kaum in die ausgereifteren europäischen Systeme der Zurechnungsbegrenzung hineinpasst.

Zu dem Fehlen eines Gesamtkonzepts und damit einer europäischen Rechts*ordnung* im wahren Sinn des Wortes kommt noch hinzu, dass die Qualität der Richtlinien schon für sich betrachtet vielfach zu wünschen übrig lässt, da nicht einmal die einzelnen Richtlinien auf durchdachten Konzepten und einem dogmatisch nachvollziehbaren Gedanken beruhen. Das könnte anschaulich an der Richtlinie über die *Produkthaftung* aus dem Jahre 1985 gezeigt werden.

In den einleitenden Erwägungen der Richtlinie findet sich der eindeutige Satz: „Die Haftung darf sich nur auf bewegliche Sachen erstrecken, die industriell hergestellt werden." Die von der Richtlinie vorgesehene verschuldensunabhängige Haftung für fehlerhafte Produkte, sollte daher – wie auch die vorhergehenden wissenschaftlichen Diskussionen zeigen – den Erwerbern Schutz vor den mit der industriellen Massenfertigung verbundenen besonderen Risken durch „Ausreißer" bieten. Das kann in der Sache damit gerechtfertigt werden, dass es trotz aller zumutbaren Maßnahmen nicht erreichbar ist, bei der industriellen Fertigung die ausnahmslose Fehlerfreiheit aller Erzeugnisse oder zumindest, bevor sie in den Verkehr gebracht werden, ein Ausscheiden der fehlerhaften Produkte durch Kontrollen zu erreichen. Im Text der Richtlinie ist jedoch die Beschränkung auf die industriellen Erzeugnisse gefallen, so dass die Haftung auch für handwerkliche, künstlerische und nunmehr auch landwirtschaftliche Erzeugnisse gilt. Die Anordnung einer Haftung, die der ausdrücklich gegebenen Begründung widerspricht und keine sonstige sachliche Rechtfertigung erkennen lässt, ist höchst problematisch.

Derartige Mängel und Widersprüche führen dazu, dass sich das Gemeinschaftsrecht aber auch die vom EU-Recht infizierten nationalen Rechtsordnungen immer weiter von einem dogmatisch durchdachten, in sich geschlossenen System, das Gleiches gleich sowie Ungleiches ungleich behandelt, entfernen und damit zunehmend weniger dem anzustrebenden *Gerechtigkeitsideal* entsprechen.

### *Die Notwendigkeit eines europäischen Gesamtkonzepts*

Diesen Missständen kann letztlich wohl nur durch die Entwicklung eines haftungsrechtlichen Gesamtkonzeptes auf europäischer Ebene abgeholfen werden. Selbst wenn es in nächster Zeit nicht zu einem europäischen Zivilgesetzbuch kommen sollte, wäre ein derartiges Grundkonzept nicht nur für das Vertragsrecht sondern auch für das Schadenersatzrecht als Basis für die immer dichter werdende Durchsetzung mit Richtlinien, Verordnungen und Gerichtsentscheidungen nötig. Nur dadurch kann die Widersprüchlichkeit vermieden und eine den Gerechtigkeitsanforderungen entsprechende neue europäische Rechtsebene gestaltet werden.

Ein europäisches Gesamtkonzept kann aber nicht nur die erforderliche Grundlage für Richtlinien der Europäischen Union, sondern auch für Neukodifikationen nationaler Rechtsordnungen bilden; darüber hinaus könnte es auch über die Beeinflussung der Lehre und der Rechtsprechung in den Mitgliedsländern der Gemeinschaft ein allmähliches Angleichen der unterschiedlichen europäischen Rechtssysteme von innen her bewirken. Eine derartige Vereinheitlichung von innen her hätte gegenüber einer von der Europäischen Union geschaffenen Rechtsquelle sicherlich den Nachteil, dass sie nur allmählich vor sich ginge. Sie hätte aber andererseits den Vorteil, dass ein plötzlicher Bruch mit der bisherigen Tradition vermieden würde und die Akzeptanz in den einzelnen Ländern dadurch auch sicherlich erhöht würde.

Der Verwirklichung des Wunsches nach Entwicklung eines gemeinsamen, von allen Mitgliedsländern akzeptierten Gesamtkonzepts, insbesondere auch des Schadenersatzrechts, stehen allerdings erhebliche *Schwierigkeiten* entgegen. Zunächst sind doch tief greifende Unterschiede der Rechtsordnungen zu überbrücken. Dafür nur ein Beispiel, nämlich die verschuldensunabhängige Haftung für gefährliche Sachen.

Der Abschnitt über die Gefährdungshaftung war wohl jener, der innerhalb der European Group on Tort Law am heftigsten diskutiert wurde. Die Schwierigkeiten, in diesem Gebiet auf europäischer Ebene zu einer gemeinsamen Linie zu finden, sind darauf zurückzuführen, dass hier die Unterschiede zwischen den europäischen Rechtsordnungen[14] größer sind als im Bereich der Verschuldenshaftung. Die Skala beginnt bei der weitreichenden verschuldensunabhängigen Haftung des „*gardien*" im französischen Recht: Der „Halter" einer Sache hat für jeden durch die Sache verursachten Schaden

---

[14] Siehe dazu die Länderberichte und den vergleichenden Bericht in Bernhard A. KOCH/ Helmut KOZIOL (eds), Unification of Tort Law: Strict Liability, The Hague-London-Boston 2002.

unabhängig von jeglichem Verschulden einzustehen. Die Ergebnisse sind eindrucksvoll und geeignet, bei auswärtigen Juristen Erstaunen auszulösen: Ein kleines Kind, das auf dem Fensterbrett zeichnete, fiel mit seinem Bleistift in der Hand aus dem Fenster und verletzte beim Herabfallen mit dem spitzen Bleistift einen Fußgänger; die französischen Gerichte bejahten die Haftung des Kindes als „*gardien*" des Bleistiftes. Viel zurückhaltender sind die deutschsprachigen Länder, die für einzelne besondere Gefahrenquellen eine strenge, verschuldensunabhängige Haftung vorsehen; sie erfassen etwa Atomkraftwerke, Luftfahrzeuge, Kraftfahrzeuge und Rohrleitungen, eine bunte Mischung die aber jedenfalls nicht gespitzte Bleistifte umfasst. Dieses System birgt allerdings die Gefahr, dass durch die Zufälligkeit der gesetzlichen Regelung sachlich nicht gerechtfertigte Unterschiede bestehen oder gleich gefährliche Sachen oft überhaupt nicht erfasst werden und daher Gleiches nicht Gleich behandelt wird, was der Gerechtigkeit widerspricht. In Österreich wird dies durch analoge Anwendung der vorhandenen Regeln immerhin in engen Grenzen gehalten; in Deutschland wirkt sich hingegen dieses Risiko voll aus. Die Skala endet im englischen Recht, das nur mit größter Zurückhaltung Gefährdungshaftungen anerkennt und nicht einmal dem Halter von Motorfahrzeugen eine verschuldensunabhängige Haftung auferlegt. Übereinstimmung besteht zwischen den europäischen Rechtsordnungen daher nur in geringem Ausmaß, vorwiegend dort, wo internationale Konventionen oder Richtlinien der EU den Weg vorzeichnen. Dementsprechend abwechslungsreich und heftig gestaltete sich auch die Diskussion der European Group on Tort Law über die gemeinsame Linie. Sie konnte sich auch nur, aber immerhin, auf eine „kleine Generalklausel" für Quellen *außergewöhnlich hoher* Gefahren einigen, die durch nationale Einzelregeln für Quellen hoher Gefahr ergänzt werden soll. Auch diese nicht sehr befriedigende Kompromisslösung bedeutet auf europäischer Ebene wohl schon einen Fortschritt.

Neben derartigen Unterschieden sind aber überdies die recht weit auseinander gehenden Denkgewohnheiten einander anzunähern. Zu beachten ist nicht nur der Unterschied zwischen dem angelsächsischen Fallrecht und dem kontinentaleuropäischen Gesetzesrecht, sondern auch die Schwierigkeiten, die sich aus der auf unterschiedlichem Niveau liegenden juristischen Dogmatik in den mehreren Rechtskreisen angehörenden Rechtsordnungen ergeben. Ein anschauliches Beispiel bietet etwa der Unterschied zwischen dem deutschen und dem französischen Rechtsdenken: Die Deutschen differenzieren mit philosophisch geschulter dogmatischer Trennschärfe; die Franzosen neigen zwar bei den Käsesorten – angeblich 450 – zu feinsten Unterschieden, im juristischen Bereich haben sie jedoch einen ausgeprägten

Hang, unterschiedliche Haftungsvoraussetzungen zu vermengen: Verursachung, Rechtswidrigkeit, Verschulden, Schutzzweck der Norm usw werden häufig nicht ausreichend auseinandergehalten.

Bei realistischer Betrachtungsweise muss auch davon ausgegangen werden, dass ein neu geschaffenes europäisches Privatrecht nicht den Standard der heute am höchsten entwickelten nationalen Rechtsordnungen erreicht, sondern bestenfalls ein mittleres Niveau. Nicht zu vernachlässigen ist auch die Gefahr, dass durch die bei solchen internationalen Projekten fast unvermeidlichen Kompromisse kaum ein wirklich homogenes, in sich geschlossenes, einheitlichen Wertungen folgendes System entstehen wird, sondern spürbare Bruchlinien vorhanden sein werden. Die europäische Rechtsvereinheitlichung wird daher zumindest zunächst bedauerlicherweise für die höher entwickelten Rechtsordnungen zu einer gewissen Niveausenkung und auch zu einem Verlust an Rechtskultur führen. Es soll aber durch eine möglichst gründliche Vorbereitung der Rechtsvereinheitlichung durch die Zusammenarbeit aller interessierten Kreise versucht werden, die negativen Auswirkungen möglichst gering zu halten. Die *European Group on Tort Law*, die bei der Forschungsstelle für Europäisches Privatrecht eine Heimstätte gefunden hat, hat ganz in diesem Sinn Prinzipien eines einheitlichen Europäischen Schadenersatzrechts ausgearbeitet und damit eine wesentliche Vorarbeit geleistet[15].

## *Zusammenfassung*

Die Rechtsangleichung ist eine Notwendigkeit; sie wird in nächster Zeit vielleicht eher als Übel empfunden werden, da sie nur punktuell sowie ohne Konzept durchgeführt wird und damit auch eine Rechtszersplitterung bewirkt. Andererseits: Durch das Lernen von einander, das Aufnehmen von Gedanken aus allen Rechtsordnungen kann sie nach einer schwierigen Anfangszeit zu einer Bereicherung unseres Rechtsdenkens und der Fortentwicklung führen. Sie ist daher auch eine große Chance. Wir müssen uns aber mit allen Kräften darum bemühen, sie zu nützen. Das positive Bemühen ist zwar erheblich schwieriger als das Kritisieren, aber auch befriedigender, da es der einzige Weg zum Fortschritt und zur Verwirklichung einer großen Idee ist: Einem Europa des Miteinander und nicht des Gegeneinander.

---

[15] EUROPEAN GROUP ON TORT LAW, Principles of European Tort Law. Text and Commentary, Wien-New York 2005.

# Europas Einheit durch Recht

## Eine politikwissenschaftliche Betrachtung der europäischen Rechtsgemeinschaft

SONJA PUNTSCHER-RIEKMANN*

### *Einleitung*

Es war der erste europäische Kommissionspräsident Walter Hallstein, der für die Europäische Wirtschaftsgemeinschaft den Begriff der Rechtsgemeinschaft geprägt hat[1]. Das Wort ist Programm: Von der Kohle- und Stahlgemeinschaft bis zur Europäischen Union setzen die Europäer auf das Recht als Mittel zur Friedenssicherung durch zwischenstaatliche Kooperation und Integration in allen Politikfeldern. Aus dem Vertragsrecht wächst der Korpus des Sekundärrechts und auf der Grundlage beider die Judikatur des Europäischen Gerichtshofs. Dieses Recht hat Vorrang vor nationalem Recht. Harmonisierung und gegenseitige Anerkennung von Rechtsnormen der Mitgliedstaaten sind Strategien der Integration des Rechts und durch das Recht. „Integration through Law" heißt ein umfassend angelegter Vergleich des europäischen mit dem US-amerikanischen Integrationsprozess aus den achtziger Jahren des vorigen Jahrhunderts: „Integration is not a simple exercise in power-sharing, but goes deeper and aims at a fundamental restructuring of society and societal attitudes, and these changes are reflected in and promoted by the law"[2], schreiben die Autoren in einem Kapitel, das Integration durch Recht mit dem Ziel einer europäischen Identitätsbildung verknüpft. Es ist das Leitbild einer modernen Vision von Politik, die nicht auf Gewalt, sondern wesentlich auf das Recht setzt. Das Bild rekurriert auf eine europäische Geschichte, in der von der hellenischen und besonders der römischen

* Damalige Direktorin des Instituts für Europäische Integrationsforschung (EIF), Österreichische Akademie der Wissenschaften, Wien, Österreich.

[1] Jürgen GRUNWALD, Die EG als Rechtsgemeinschaft, in: Moritz RÖTTINGER/Claudia WEYRINGER (Hg), Handbuch der Europäischen Integration, Wien 1991, 15

[2] Mauro CAPPELLETTI/Monica SECCOMBE/Joseph WEILER, Integration through Law, vol 1, Book 1, Berlin-New York 1986, 43.

über die mittelalterliche bis herauf zur neuzeitlichen rechtsstaatlichen Praxis das Recht eine zentrale Rolle in der sozialen Ordnung spielt. Es ist geprägt von der Vorstellung einer Evolution von Gesellschaft als zivilisatorischem Prozess, in dem das Recht am besten dazu in der Lage ist, menschlichen Differenzen und deren historischer Kontingenz angemessen zu begegnen. In der Tat baut die seit mehr als einem halben Jahrhundert andauernde europäische Suche nach Einheit wesentlich auf das Recht, das sich vom klassischen Völkerrecht allmählich zu innerstaatlichem Recht entwickelt hat. In dieser Logik steht die heutige Debatte um eine europäische Verfassung. Damit konsistent ist das Insistieren der Europäer auf den Respekt des Völkerrechts in internationalen Krisen.

Ausgehend von einer bis zur Antike zurückreichenden europäischen Tradition, in der das Recht stets eine zivilisierende Rolle in den politischen und gesellschaftlichen Machtkämpfen beanspruchte, will dieser Artikel die Dimension des Rechts für den heutigen europäischen Einigungsprozess ausloten. Besondere Beachtung findet darin die Entstehung des europäischen Konstitutionalismus aus dem Primär- und Sekundärrecht der Union und dessen Infragestellung in der Auseinandersetzung um das Telos von Integration. Die folgenden philosophisch-historischen Skizzen sind nicht Selbstzweck, sie dienen der Erinnerung an eine europäische Tradition, die insofern identitätsstiftend sein könnte, als das Ringen um eine Rechtsordnung alle europäische Gesellschaften und Staaten verbindet.

## *Zur Dialektik von Integration und Recht*

Recht gibt es, weil es Dissens gibt. Dissens ist die Folge der Pluralität von Menschen. Doch gilt diese an sich triviale Wahrheit nicht unabhängig von Gesellschaftsformationen und den darin dominierenden Menschenbildern und Ordnungsvorstellungen. In vormodernen Stammesgesellschaften mit ihren stabilen Verwandtschaftsbeziehungen, in denen das Individuum sich durch seinen Status in diesen Beziehungen definiert, existieren andere Rechtsvorstellungen als in komplexen Gesellschaften, deren zentrales Kennzeichnen die soziale Mobilität der Einzelnen ist. Die britische Rechtshistoriker Sir Henry Sumner Maine hat die Entwicklung des Rechts von Stammesgesellschaften zum römischen Recht als „movement from status to contract“ bezeichnet. Der Mobilität der Menschen und der Steigerung der Komplexität von Beziehungen entspricht die Mobilisierung der Rechtsverhältnisse. Was die Römer „erfunden“ haben, ist in der Moderne zur kleinen Münze des Gesellschaftsverkehrs geworden: „Damit entfällt die Anknüpfung der Rechtsverteilung an eine zu konkret fixierte Gesellschaftsstruktur.

Das neue Verteilungsmittel heißt Vertrag. Es setzt nach liberaler Auffassung nur noch klare Typen zur Erleichterung rascher Verständigung zwischen Unbekannten, Vorschriften gegen wechselseitige Schädigung und berechenbar funktionierende Gerichtsbarkeit voraus. In diesem Rahmen könne die Gesellschaft Beliebiges tolerieren."[3] Die Bewegung vom Status zum Vertrag ist eine zentrale Errungenschaft der westlichen Rechtskultur, die sowohl den Vertrag zwischen Privaten als auch den Vertrag zwischen Herrschern und Beherrschten durch die Konstituierung von öffentlicher Macht und Gewalt hervorbringt.

Wandel und Anpassung von Normen und Regeln ist nicht das Wesen, sondern das historische Schicksal des Rechts, dessen Logik eigentlich darin besteht, Menschen an gleiche und dauerhafte Regeln zu binden, um ihr Zusammenleben zu ermöglichen, zu zivilisieren und zu stabilisieren. Luhmann spricht von Erwartungssicherheit: „Die Funktion des Rechts hat es mit Erwartungen zu tun; und zwar wenn man auf Gesellschaften und nicht nur auf Individuen abstellt, mit der Möglichkeit, Erwartungen zu kommunizieren und in der Kommunikation zur Anerkennung zu bringen."[4] Dies ist die Funktion, die das Recht auch im internationalen und noch viel mehr supranationalen Kontext erfüllt. Dass europäische Integration so eng mit der Rechtsentwicklung und schließlich mit dem Entstehen einer eigenen neuen Rechtsordnung verknüpft ist, beruht auf der Tatsache, dass die Mitgliedstaaten der Union einander besonders misstrauen, oder zumindest in der Vergangenheit misstrauten, und Kooperation nur dann einzugehen bereit sind, wenn ihre Souveränitätsabgabe an supranationale Institutionen mit der Erfüllung (oder wenigstens der Option auf Erfüllung) von Erwartungen kompensiert wird. Diese Erwartungen sind primär sozio-ökonomischer Natur, wie Moravcsik gezeigt hat[5], doch gesellen sich heute mehr denn je auch sicherheitspolitische Aspekte dazu. In keinem Bereich ist europäische Politik so schnell gewachsen wie in der dritten Säule seit dem Gipfel von Tampere 1999.[6]

---

3 Niklas LUHMANN, Rechtssoziologie, Opladen 1987, 15.

4 Niklas LUHMANN, Das Recht der Gesellschaft, Frankfurt a.M. 1997, 125.

5 Andrew MORAVCSIK, The Choice for Europe. Social Purpose and State Power from Messina to Maastricht, London: UCL 1998.

6 Jörg MONAR, Decision-making in the Area of Freedom, Security, and Justice, in Anthony ARNULL/Daniel WINCOTT (eds) Accountability and Legitimacy in the European Union, Oxford University Press 2002, 63–80 und Jörg MONAR, 'Justice and Home Affairs', Journal of Common Market Studies 2005/43, 131–46.

## *Europäische Rechtstradition: „Von Bologna bis Brüssel"?*

Vielleicht ließe sich in einer weiteren Übertreibung von Jacques Le Goffs Übertreibung der Bedeutung des Mittelalters[7] für alle nachfolgenden Epochen die ewige Bedeutung der Antike hervorheben, zumal ja die mit einem Bein im Mittelalter stehenden Revolutionäre des Humanismus und der Renaissance ihre Position mit neuen Lektüren und Aneignungen der antiken Autoren begründeten. Die Autoren der amerikanischen und französischen Revolution des 18. Jahrhunderts schwelgen jedenfalls in Begeisterung für die athenische Polis und die römische Republik, wenn Thomas Paine hofft, „Amerika wird in vergrößertem Maßstab sein, was Athen in Miniatur war", und Saint-Just theatralisch ausruft: „Seit den Römern war die Welt leer, erfüllt nur mit Erinnerungen an sie, die jetzt uns prophetisch die Freiheit ankündigen".[8] Doch was wir von Übertreibung zu Übertreibung gewinnen können, ist vielleicht nur diese eine Erkenntnis: Dass die Europäer Entdecker und Wiederentdecker sind, dass ihre kulturelle Leistung in einer „permanenten Revolution" des Gefundenen durch Selektion und Vermischung besteht, dass sie mit einer gewissen Nonchalance ältere und fremde Kulturen zu ihren Ahnen machen, ohne deren Setzungen je zur Gänze zu übernehmen. Im Gegenteil: „Die gleichen Formulierungen hatten ganz verschiedene Bedeutung", schreibt Berman über die Wiederentdeckung des römischen Rechts und dessen Integration in das Rechtssystem der freien Stadt Pisa im 12. Jahrhundert.[9] In diesem Sinne ist wohl auch die von Coing auf die europäische Rechtsgeschichte gemünzte Formel von „Bologna bis Brüssel" zu verstehen, mit der eine Kontinuität des Rechts und der Rezeptionspraxis beschworen wird: „Europa findet, gewinnt und verstärkt unbewusst seine Identität durch Wellen immer neuer auf das Recht bezogener Rezeptions- und Produktionsvorgänge, die wie Kraftlinien in die Welt ausgreifen", schreibt Häberle in seiner Europäischen Rechtskultur, und weiter: „...Europa durchlebt heute selbst eine einzigartige *Europäisierung in der Weise des Rechts*, die den Blick auf ältere Perioden des ‚gemeinen Rechts' des europäischen Mittelalters *vor* der Zeit des klassischen Nationalstaates zurücklenkt."[10] Dies ist eine Rede, die

[7] Jacques LE GOFF, L'Europe est-elle née au Moyen Age?, Paris 2003.

[8] Beide zitiert bei Hannah ARENDT, Über die Revolution, München 1986, 253. John Adams reiht sich ebenfalls in diese Euphorie ein mit dem Satz „dass die römische Verfassung das edelste Volk geprägt und die größte Macht erzeugt hat, die je existierte." (ebda)

[9] Harold J. BERMAN, Recht und Revolution. Die Bildung der westlichen Rechtstradition, Frankfurt a.M. 1995, 17f.

[10] Peter HÄBERLE, Europäische Rechtskultur, Frankfurt a.M. 1997, 11 (Hervorhebungen im Original). Vgl auch Häberles Kommentar der Coingschen Formel „von Bologna bis

wohl gegen all jene gehalten wird, die diesen Prozess mit der Betonung der Verschiedenheit der mitgliedstaatlichen Rechtsordnungen in Frage stellen wollen. Die Insistenz auf diese Differenz war und bleibt unter anderem die conditio sine qua non der Nationalstaatlichkeit. Die rhetorisch-strategische Insistenz ist bis auf den heutigen Tag erfolgreich. Umso bemerkenswerter ist, dass ausgerechnet zwei englische Autoren weit vor der europäischen Einigung den „Isolationismus" der englischen Juristen als unzulässige Übertreibung kritisierten: Edmund Burke im 18. und Frederic William Maitland im 19. Jahrhundert.[11] Doch die Behauptung der Unvergleichbarkeit der europäischen Rechtsordnungen durch unterlassenen Vergleich ist nicht nur eine britische Spezialität. Rechtsvergleichung ist überall eine unterrepräsentierte Disziplin. Dass Kimmel im Jahre 2000 in einer vergleichenden Untersuchung der Verfassungen der EU-Mitgliedstaaten zu dem Schluss kommt, „dass hinsichtlich der wichtigsten Verfassungsprinzipien und grundlegenden Verfassungsstrukturen ein hohes Maß an Homogenität herrscht"[12], kann den Historiker wohl kaum überraschen, resultieren diese Prinzipien doch aus der europäischen Revolutionsgeschichte, die in England nach der Magna Charta von 1215 im 17. Jahrhundert noch einmal beginnt, sich in Frankreich im 18. fortsetzt und von hier aus den ganzen Kontinent erfasst. Dass die

---

Brüssel": „Er (Coing) zieht damit die Linie aus bzw. zurück bis Rom, und wenn wir heute von ‚Gemeineuropäischem Zivilrecht' bzw. ‚Gemeinsamen Privatrecht in der Europäischen Gemeinschaft', von ‚ius commune europaeum publicum' bzw. ‚Gemeineuropäischem Verfassungsrecht' sprechen, wenn allenthalben eine ‚Europäisierung' der juristischen Teilgebiete beobachtet und befördert wird (beginnend mit dem ‚Europäischen Verwaltungsrecht' bis hin zum Europäischen Sozial- und Arbeitsrecht und gipfelnd in dem Desiderat einer ‚europäischen Juristenausbildung'), so zeigt sich darin ein Mehrfaches: In Europa hat eine neue Phase begonnen; die begrenzte Relativierung des Nationalstaates bzw. die Europäische Einigung geschieht im Wege des Rechts..." (ebda, 10 f; siehe auch die dort angegebene Literatur).

[11] Burke sagte einmal: „Die Gesetze aller europäischen Nationen leiten sich aus denselben Quellen her", während Maitland in seiner Antrittsvorlesung 1888 in Cambridge den Mangel einer englischen Rechtsgeschichte beklagte und diesen Mangel auf eine Unfähigkeit des englischen Juristen zum Vergleich zurückführte: „dem englischen Juristen, der nichts kannte und sich für nichts interessierte als sein eigenes System, (kam) der Gedanke der Rechtsgeschichte kaum in den Sinn....Einer der Gründe, warum man sich so wenig um unser mittelalterliches Recht gekümmert hat, ist nach meiner Überzeugung unsere gründliche und seit langem geheiligte Unkenntnis des französischen und deutschen Rechts. Die englischen Juristen haben in den letzten sechs Jahrhunderten die Unvergleichbarkeit unserer Rechtsgeschichte übertrieben..." (beide zitiert nach Harold J. Berman (wie Anm 9) 40 f).

[12] Verfassungen der EU-Mitgliedstaaten. Textausgabe mit einer Einführung von Adolf Kimmel und Christiane Kimmel, 5. Aufl München 2000, xxxi.

neuen Freiheitsprinzipien mit der Idee der Nation verbunden wurden und diese sich auch in dialektischer Opposition zum napoleonischen Revolutionsexport entwickelte, macht es bis heute so schwierig, zu den gemeinsamen Wurzeln zurückzukehren.[13]

Die Skeptiker des europäischen Integrationsprozesses begreifen jedenfalls, dass es sich hierbei um eine zwar leise, aber doch auch um eine Revolution handelt, die Europa grundlegend verändert und sich dafür des Rechts bedient. Vorrang und Direktwirkung des europäischen Rechts, dessen Adressat nicht nur der Mitgliedstaat, sondern auch der Bürger und die Bürgerin ist, sind der prominenteste Ausdruck dieser Revolution, die in Form von EuGH-Judikaten und nicht von vertraglichen Abkommen der Mitgliedstaaten daherkommt[14]. Aus diesem Grunde ist die Beschwörung der Vergangenheit durch die „Revolutionäre“ eine strategische Operation, die sich durchaus in eine Tradition europäischer Revolutionsdiskurse einordnet. Mit Blick auf die gregorianische Revolution schreibt Berman: „Der Mythos von der Rückkehr zu einer älteren Zeit ist freilich das Kennzeichen aller europäischen Revolutionen“.[15] Interessant ist jedenfalls, dass in Häberles oder Coings Argumentation die Vergangenheit zum Fundus der neuen europäischen Rechtsordnung wird, so wie im frühen Mittelalter die Kanonisten im Rückgriff auf den *Corpus Iuris Iustiniani* als „ratio scripta“ das „ius novum“ der Kirche rechtfertigten. Dieser Rückgriff diente zunächst der Kirche zur Systematisierung des eigenen Rechts, während die Kaiser des heiligen römischen Reiches den *Corpus iuris* als Legitimationsquelle ihrer Reichsidee gegen die widerstrebenden Fürsten benutzten. Und diese wiederum verwendeten aus demselben Korpus, was ihnen in der Abwehr des kaiserlichen Machtanspruches brauchbar erschien.[16]

---

[13] Nur als Anekdote sei hier erwähnt, dass ich mich zu Beginn eines Seminars zum Vergleich der europäischen Verfassungen an der Humboldt-Universität zu Berlin im Wintersemester 2000 mit gänzlich ungläubigen Studierenden konfrontiert sah, die am Ende der gemeinsamen Lektüre und Diskussion über die Verfassungen der 15 EU-Mitgliedstaaten und ausgewählter osteuropäischer Beitrittskandidaten durchaus von unseren gemeinsamen Wurzeln überzeugt waren.

[14] Siehe dazu Maurizio BACH, Eine leise Revolution durch Verwaltungsverfahren, Bürokratische Organisationsprozesse in der Europäischen Gemeinschaft, in: Zeitschrift für Soziologie 21, 1, 16–30; Anne-Marie BURLEY/Walter MATTLI, Europe before the Court, A Political theory of Legal Integration, in: International Organization 47/1, 41–76; Sonja PUNTSCHER RIEKMANN, Die kommissarische Neuordnung Europas. Das Dispositiv der Integration, Wien-New York 1998.

[15] Harold J. BERMAN (wie Anm 9) 37.

[16] Paul KOSCHAKER, Europa und das römische Recht, München-Berlin 1966.

Ein weiterer aus heutiger Sicht bemerkenswerter Aspekt der gregorianischen Revolution ist die Idee verschränkter oder besser einander beschränkender Souveränitäten, die keinem, weder dem weltlichen, noch dem geistlichen Herrscher höchste und absolute Macht zugestand. Jeder fand seine Grenze an der Jurisdiktion des anderen, soweit diese rechtmäßig war, und „jeder Staat existierte in einem System pluraler Jurisdiktionen".[17] Noch war das später alles dominierende Dogma der unverletzlichen Souveränität des Staates nach innen wie nach außen gebannt. Ebenso die Idee der absoluten zentralistischen Macht des Königs oder des Staates. Innerstaatlich wie zwischenstaatlich wohnte diesen Rechtsvorstellungen zivilisatorisches, weil befriedendes Potential inne.

Doch die Geschichte Europas, die nach der Renaissance immer deutlicher eine Geschichte der säkularen, sich nach innen zentralisierenden und nach außen abgrenzenden Staaten mit imaginierten homogenen Volksgemeinschaften sein wird, ist eine Geschichte von Aufbruch und Niedergang, von großen Anstrengungen auf der Suche nach Wegen, die Menschen aus Unmündigkeit und Unterdrückung zu befreien, um sie dann umso grausamer in tiefste Abhängigkeit und unter das Joch totaler Herrschaft zurückzustoßen. Es ist Europas Geschichte mit ihren hellen und dunklen Seiten. Das Recht blieb davon nicht verschont: Es hatte seine Rolle in hellen wie in dunklen Zeiten und Juristen fanden ihre Rolle in allen Regimen.

Bedeutsam ist aber, dass Europa im Laufe der Geschichte immer wieder von einem Pluralismus geprägt war, der trotz aller Verengungen und Totalitätsansprüche sich auch durch die dunkelsten Zeiten Europas erhalten hat und stets eine (wenn auch manchmal nur ideelle) Quelle von Freiheit blieb. Berman jedenfalls sieht in der Koexistenz und Konkurrenz verschiedener Rechtsprechungen und Rechtssysteme in derselben Gesellschaft die vielleicht „kennzeichnendste Eigenschaft der westlichen Rechtstradition...Und diese Pluralität ... macht die Herrschaft des Rechts einmal notwendig und zum anderen auch möglich."[18]

### *Pluralität und Einheit durch Recht und Demokratie: Die Europäische Union als „constitutio libertatis"*

Die Europäische Union ist auch Erbin dieser Tradition. Christian Joerges beschreibt die europäische Verfassungsordnung als Unitas in Pluralitate. Sie ist ihm das zentrale Merkmal des europäischen Rechts als Konsequ-

[17] Harold J. Berman (wie Anm 9) 468.
[18] Harold J. Berman (wie Anm 9) 28f.

enz der Komplexität europäischen Regierens, „in which decisions are neither delegated to supranational expert bodies nor entrusted to the European Commission, but cannot be referred back to national parliamentary bodies either, or brought under the ultimate responsibility of the European Parliament.“[19] Man mag dem phänomenologisch zustimmen, doch gerade diese schillernde Situation von komplexen Zuständigkeiten und Verantwortlichkeiten schafft Probleme der politischen Akzeptanz. Der 2007 zur Verhandlung vorliegende Vertrag, der an Stelle des gescheiterten Verfassungsvertrages EUV und EGV ändern soll, wird die Komplexität nicht reduzieren, sondern durch eine Reihe von wichtigen Bestimmungen wie etwa jene zum Vorrang des europäischen Rechts oder zum unverfälschten Wettbewerb in Protokolle verschieben. Natürlich kann und muss man fragen, ob die zahlreichen europäischen Differenzen, die man etwas euphemistisch als Vielfalt bezeichnet, eine Komplexitätsreduktion überhaupt zulassen. Doch hätte der Verfassungsvertrag im Bereich der Institutionenordnung und der Grundrechte ein größeres Maß an Klarheit gebracht, die nun wieder geopfert wird. Es bleibt offen, ob jene Bevölkerungen, die auch in Falle des neuen Vertrages zum Referendum aufgerufen sind, diesem ihre Zustimmung erteilen werden.

Die Union steht an einem Wendepunkt, der, so die These dieses Artikels, nach einem Gründungsakt verlangt, um ihre Macht nach innen zu legitimieren und nach außen zu beweisen, in dem die oben skizzierte Geschichte europäischer Politik- und Rechtstraditionen inspirierend sein mag, der Akt selbst bedarf des politischen Willens, der nicht aus dem Recht kommt. Der Wille aber wird nur aus der Not geboren. Die Not, die Europa heute treibt, ist die Erweiterung der Union auf 27 Mitglieder und deren Integration. Der Ausweg wurde zuletzt in einem Verfassungskonvent gesucht. Er hat im Juni 2003 einen neuen Verfassungsentwurf vorgelegt, doch blieb ihm bis jetzt der endgültige Erfolg versagt. Doch die Geschichte lehrt uns, dass Verfassungsgebungen noch stets zu den größten und daher gefährlichsten Unternehmen politischer Gemeinschaften gehörten. Wir vergessen oder verdrängen nicht nur die Tatsache, dass die nationalen Verfassungsprozesse in Europa großen Auseinandersetzungen und oft blutigen Kämpfen geschuldet waren, sondern auch jene, dass die allgemein bewunderte US-Verfassung nach den Worten von John Adams nur mit äußerster Mühe „unter dem Druck bitterster Notwendigkeit einer höchst widerwilligen Nation hat abgezwungen“ werden

[19] Christian JOERGES, Integration through de-legalisation? An irritated heckler. European Governance Papers (EUROGOV) No N-07–03, <http://www.connex-network.org/eurogov/pdf/egp-newgov-N-07-03.pdf> 17.

können.[20] Wohl deshalb wurde das einmal vollbrachte Werk über Nacht zum Gegenstand „einer unkritischen und fast blinden Anbetung“, wie Wilson später sagen würde.[21] Warum soll dies in Europa nicht möglich sein?

Ein Ziel dieses Artikels ist es zu zeigen, dass die europäische Zivilisationsgeschichte engstens mit ihrer Rechtsgeschichte verknüpft ist. Ein wesentlicher Aspekt dieser Rechtsgeschichte ist das Verfassungsrecht. Die großen europäischen Auseinandersetzungen fanden um die Verfassung, die constitutio libertatis, statt, nicht um das Privatrecht. Letzteres entwickelte sich auch aus Differenzen, jener von Privaten, und sorgte für geordnete Verkehrsformen zwischen diesen, aber es war nicht Thema und Motiv von Revolutionen. Es entstand „organischer“, als Antwort auf Erfahrungen, die mit ökonomischen Entwicklungen zu tun hatten und meinte eine Sicherheit des Vertrags mit dem Partner. Der Verfassungskampf war dagegen auf die Alles andere grundlegende Ordnung gerichtet. Noch der Kampf um soziale Rechte richtet sich auf die Herrschaft, mithin auf den Staat, weil es zunächst um die Berechtigung von Bürgern ging, diesen Kampf überhaupt zu führen. Auch der Kampf des bürgerlichen Dritten Standes im 18. Jahrhundert ist nicht ein Kampf der neuen Reichen aus ökonomischen Motiven (sie waren ja trotz der illiberalen Ordnung reich geworden), sondern einer aus politischen Gründen um Repräsentations- und Mitspracherechte im Entscheidungsprozeß. Der homo oeconomicus hat den homo politicus wenn nicht zur Voraussetzung, so doch zum notwendigen Korrelat. Das Schlagwort „No taxation without representation“ der amerikanischen Revolutionäre meint Repräsentation im englischen Parlament. Hätte die englische Krone nachgegeben, wäre es vielleicht nie zum Unabhängigkeitskrieg gekommen, wenigstens nicht an diesem Punkt der Geschichte.

Ein weiteres Ziel dieses Artikels ist zu zeigen, dass europäische Zivilisationsgeschichte engstens mit ihrer Demokratiegeschichte verknüpft ist und dass diese von höchster Bedeutung für ihre Rechtsgeschichte ist. Von der athenischen Polis über die römische Republik und die italienischen Stadtrepubliken bis zur modernen Demokratien gibt es einen Entwicklungsfaden, der nie abreißt, sondern verschwindet im Knäuel anderer Herrschaftsdiskurse. Tyrannis, Absolutismus, Totalitarismus: in dieser dunklen europäischen Geschichte setzt sich der Wille zur Freiheit als *basso continuo* fort, um an entscheidenden Stellen als *forte* und *fortissimo* hervorzubrechen. Immer wieder in Revolutionen, die nicht nur glücklich endeten. Im Gegenteil. Es ist wichtig, die europäischen Revolutionen und ihre Schrecken zu studieren,

---

[20] Zitiert nach Hannah Arendt (wie Anm 8) 255.

[21] Ebda.

um zu begreifen, wie groß die Aufgabe der heutigen Europäischen Union ist, ihr Verfassungsfundament zu erneuern. Nicht mehr aber auch nicht weniger war der Entwurf des Verfassungskonvents: Er ist eine maßvolle Fortentwicklung der Verträge.

Die Qualität einer politischen und rechtlichen Gemeinschaft entsteht nicht aus der Beschwörung der Vergangenheit und man könnte auch die „Vergesslichkeit“ der europäischen Staats- und Regierungschefs als angenehme Nüchternheit willkommen heißen. Doch zeigen die Debatte um die Erwähnung des Christengottes in der Verfassung und die Betonung der kulturellen Vielfalt und des Stolzes auf die nationale Identität in der Präambel, dass von Nüchternheit keine Rede sein kann. Dagegen klingt die Wiederaufnahme antiker Politik- und Rechtsdiskurse weit nüchterner und der Realität der europäischen Rechtsgemeinschaft angemessener. Sowohl der griechische Begriff „nomos“ als auch der römische Begriff „lex“ zeigen Argumentationslinien auf, die auf den künstlichen, weltlichen Charakter des Gesetzes verweisen. Etymologisch meint „lex“ die Bindung zwischen Dingen oder Menschen. In diesem Sinne gebraucht auch Montesquieu das Wort „loi“ als „rapport“. Und darum geht es im heutigen Europa wie in allen politischen Gemeinschaften: die Bindung von Verschiedenen zu einem Ganzen. Das Bündnis der Europäer kann sich weniger denn je auf irgendeiner, wie immer imaginierten Volksgemeinschaft, sondern nur auf dem freiwillig geschlossenen Vertrag gründen. Der Zirkelschluss der Integrations- und Verfassungsgegner, es könne keine Verfassung geben, weil es kein europäisches Volk gibt, entsteht aus der Leugnung des „Natur“ des Politischen wie des Rechts: Dass beide ihre Notwendigkeit der Verschiedenheit von Menschen und ihrem Dissens schulden.

Die eigentliche Problematik der Verfassungsdebatte liegt woanders, nämlich in der Frage, wie wir den Verschiedenen Stimme und Repräsentanz im europäischen Entscheidungsprozeß geben, ob dies besser durch den Rat oder das Parlament oder durch welches interinstitutionelle Zusammenspiel gewährleistet ist. Auf diese Frage hätte der Konvent eine tragfähige Antwort gefunden, die den Rat und das Parlament zum gemeinsamen Gesetzgeber für alle europäischen Gesetze (zum ersten Mal werden Rechtsakte der Union auch in einem Vertrag so bezeichnet) machte (Artikel 33 des Entwurfs). Dennoch ist der Mangel an Vertrauen der europäischen Bürger und Bürgerinnen in die europäischen Institutionen ein Stachel im Fleisch der Union. Das drückt sich vor allem in den niedrigen Beteiligungsraten in den Wahlen zum Europäischen Parlament aus. Eine jüngste Umfrage in Österreich zeigt, dass die Bürger dieses Landes in der Bedeutungshierarchie von Wahlen jene zum Europäischen Parlament mit 27% ganz unten reihen, während sie den

Gemeinderatswahlen die höchste Priorität einräumen. Die europäischen Eliten können bei der Konstruktion der Union bis jetzt nicht auf das bauen, was für John Adams in der amerikanischen Revolution und Verfassungsgebung ausschlaggebend war: Was „den Vereinigten Staaten ermöglichte, durch eine Revolution zu gehen, war das Vertrauen zwischen uns und in das gemeine Volk".[22]

In Europa misstrauen die Eliten dem Volk und dieses den Eliten. Das hat auch mit der europäischen Revolutionsgeschichte zu tun, in der das Volk zunächst heilig gesprochen und, dann, als man die Gewalt der barrikadenstürmenden Massen sah, verdammt wurde. So folgte auf die Befreiung stets die neuerliche Unterwerfung, auf die Revolution die Restauration. Wir sind jedoch heute in Europa gar nicht mit stürmenden Massen konfrontiert, weit eher mit Bürgern, die sich auf immer kleinere Welten zurückziehen. Die oben zitierte Umfrage, in der den Gemeinderatswahlen größte Bedeutung zukommt, zeugt davon. Diese Welt ist überschaubar, in ihr glaubt man noch eine Stimme zu haben, während man nicht nur Europa, sondern auch der Nation den Rücken kehrt. Doch die Stadt und die Gemeinde, jene Keimzellen der europäischen Demokratie seit der griechischen Antike, verlieren zunehmend an Steuerungsfähigkeit in sich globalisierenden Märkten. Ihre Renaissance als kulturelle Einheiten kann nur in einem größeren Rahmen gelingen.[23] Doch die Konstruktion des größeren Ganzen bedarf des Vertrauens zwischen Eliten und Volk. Nur aus diesem kann der „religiöse" Gründungsakt der neuen Einheit entstehen und auf Dauer gestellt werden.

Hannah Arendt hat das Problem des Bedarfs an Transzendenz auch für die amerikanische und französische Revolution dargestellt, ein Problem, das sie in der petitio principii erkennt: nämlich, dass die, die zusammenkommen, um den neuen Verfassungsstaat zu errichten, selber über keine verfassungsrechtliche Autorität verfügen.[24] Und sie beschreibt die Anstrengungen der Revolutionäre, nach einem „Gott", Robespierres „Höchstem Wesen" oder Adams „großem Gesetzgeber des Alls"[25] zu suchen, der ihr Unternehmen legitimieren könnte. Diese Suche blieb in diesem Sinne erfolglos, wenngleich „Vergöttlichung" des Volkes, der Nation oder des Staates der europäischen

[22] Zitiert nach Hannah Arendt (wie Anm 8) 236.

[23] Sonja Puntscher Riekmann, Urbanity and Cititzenship: Essentials of European Culture, in: Kultur der Demokratie. Festschrift für Manfried Welan zum 65. Geburtstag, Wien 2002, 83 f.

[24] Hannah Arendt (wie Anm 8) 238ff.

[25] Womit hier nicht eine Gleichstellung von Robespierre, dessen Humanismus in der „Terreur" endete, mit Adams intendiert ist, sondern nur ein Verweis auf eine gleiche Problematik.

Revolutionäre sehr wohl als säkulares Substitut funktionierte. Aber vor allem mussten sie darauf bauen, dass die von ihnen gestiftete Ordnung sich schon durchsetzen und durch Erfolg legitimieren würde. Im heutigen Europa stellt sich die Legitimationsfrage der Verfassungsgründer anders. Obwohl die Legitimität des Konvents immer wieder bezweifelt wurde, ist sie durch die Entscheidung des Europäischen Rates in Laeken (2001) durchaus gewährleistet. Der Konvent ist außerdem nur zur Ausarbeitung, nicht zur Verabschiedung der neuen Verfassung aufgerufen worden. Die Entscheidung erfolgt nach Artikel 48 des geltenden Unionsvertrages, das heißt durch Zustimmung der Staats- und Regierungschefs in einer Regierungskonferenz, durch Ratifikation in den nationalen Parlamenten und in manchen Staaten durch Referenda. Zwar handelt es sich auch in Europa um einen Konstitutionsakt, der vieles ändern wird, aber er entsteht nicht auf der tabula rasa der alten Ordnung, schon gar nicht unter dem Druck revolutionärer Bajonette. Man sollte das begrüßen.

Doch leidet dieser Vorgang zweifelsohne an einem Begeisterungsmangel. Die Bürger konnten sich mit dem Entwurf nicht identifizieren, ja sie wussten gar nichts davon. Schon der Bekanntheitsgrad des Konvents war in den meisten Staaten relativ gering und das im Zeitalter nie da gewesener medialer Kommunikation. Dass der Konvent in Artikel 1 erstmals den „Willen der Bürgerinnen und Bürger" noch vor die Staaten als Legitimationsquelle der neuen Verfassung stellt, blieb weitgehend unbekannt. Dort wo eine Verfassungsdebatte geführt wurde, dominierte die Frage, ob jeder Staat weiterhin über einen Kommissar verfügen wird oder ob die doppelten Mehrheiten im Rat zu Lasten der kleinen Staaten gehen werden. Die Debatte ist wesentlich eine um die Rolle der Nationen in Europa, nicht um Europa und seine Rolle in der Welt. Dafür bedürfte es in der Tat eines „religiösen" Bekenntnisses zur Union. Religiös im Sinne jenes römischen Verständnisses von „Religion", das „ursprünglich nicht anderes meint als das *religare*, das Sich-Zurückbinden an einen Anfang ... so dass die römische *Pietät* in der Tat darin bestand, dass man sich an den Anfang römischer Geschichte, die Gründung einer ewigen Stadt, gebunden und ihm verpflichtet fühlte."[26]

Damit allerdings die Bürger und Bürgerinnen diesen Akt des „religare" (hier muss nochmals auf die gleiche etymologische Wurzel von „lex" verwiesen werden) als eigenen betrachten, müssen sie an der Verfassung beteiligt werden, indem man diese einem europäischen Referendum unterwirft. Es wäre einfach gewesen, dies mit der Europawahl im Juni 2004 zu verknüpfen, doch man hat sich dieser Chance begeben. Aber wie sonst will

[26] Hannah ARENDT (wie Anm 8) 255 (Hervorhebungen im Original).

Europa je die Macht des amerikanischen Bewusstseins vom eigenen „novus ordo saeclorum“ begreifen. Es entstand im Gründungsakt der Verfassung, dessen Prinzip das Vertrauen auf Teilhaberschaft im Bündnis war. Alle Machtfragen sozio-ökonomischer und außenpolitischer Natur lassen sich nur auf dieser Grundlage legitimerweise entscheiden, ob es sich um eine europäische Wirtschafts- und Sozialpolitik oder um die Intervention in einem internationalen Konflikt handelt.

Solange „Europa im Nirgendwo“ liegt und seine „Identität durch die Abwesenheit jeglicher Identität“ gestiftet werden soll, wie Peter Sloterdijk und Régis Debray angesichts einer Diskussion über das abstrakte Design der Euro-Noten im Gegensatz zu den bedeutungsschwangeren Dollarnoten kritisierten[27], bleibt eine Teilhabe Europas an den großen internationalen Machtfragen prekär. Ich habe selbst vor einiger Zeit die Gesichts- und Geschichtslosigkeit des europäischen Geldes kritisiert[28]. Doch sind sie nur Epiphänome eines tieferen Dilemmas: Der Weltmachtanspruch (Laqueur) kann nicht gelingen ohne demokratisch legitimierte Vertiefung im Inneren und diese nicht ohne Identifikation der Unionsbürger mit „ihrer“ Union. Die Nicht-Identifikation der Europäer mit der neuen Polity ist Konsequenz ihrer Nicht-Beteiligung, ihrer relativen Bindungslosigkeit. Daher empfinden sie das europäische Recht oft als Oktroi (vor allem wenn es durch Mehrheitsentscheidung zustande kommt)[29] oder als übertriebenen Legalismus[30], jeden-

[27] Lorenz JÄGER, Europa liegt im Nirgendwo. Peter Sloterdijk und Régis Debray lesen Nicht-Texte, in: Frankfurter Allgemeine Zeitung, 19.2.2004, Nr. 42, 33.

[28] Sonja PUNTSCHER RIEKMANN (wie Anm 23) 85 ff.

[29] Man erinnere sich an die Empörung in Österreich über die Entscheidungen von Rat und Parlament in der Transitfrage, die medial als Empörung einer Nation über das Ausland dargestellt wurde und nur ein weiteres Schlaglicht auf die Nicht-Identifikation mit der Union, der man doch angehört, wirft. Ein anderes Problem, das wegen seiner Komplexität hier nicht behandelt werden konnte, ist jenes der Implementierung von Gemeinschaftsrecht in den nationalen Rechtsordnungen. Siehe dazu Peter SLOMINSKI, Die Implementierung des Telekommunikationsrechts in Österreich, Wien 2002 und Bedanna BAPULY/Gerhard KOHLEGGER, Die Implementierung des EG-Rechts in Österreich. Die Gerichtsbarkeit, Wien 2003, in der von mir und Michael SCHWEITZER herausgegebenen Reihe „Institutioneller Wandel und Europäische Integration“, Wien 2002/2003.

[30] Siehe dazu Paul CRAIG, The Nature of the Community: Integration, Democracy and Legitimacy, in: Paul CRAIG, Gráinne DE BÚRCA, The Evolution of EU Law, Oxford 1998, 1–54. Nun ist der Vorwurf des Legalismus nicht nur gegen die EU, sondern oft auch gegen die Nationalstaaten gerichtet. Dabei ist die Problem der EU als “regulatory state” (Majone), dass das Recht ihr wesentliches Regulationsinstrument ist, da sie über nur sehr geringe andere, vor allem Budgtemittel verfügt, die sie mit bestimmten Steuerungsabsichten einsetzen kann. Dabei ist in den letzten Jahren ohnehin ein Form des Regierens entstanden, die stärker auf „soft law“ oder „soft modes of governance“ setzt

falls kaum als Errungenschaft einer zivilisierenden Anstrengung, Frieden und Freiheit auf diesem Kontinent qua Recht zu garantieren. Dies ist für die Gemeinschaft und ihr Recht nicht ohne Gefahren, denn wenn Luhmanns Argument von der vertrauensschaffenden Funktion des Rechts richtig ist, dann ist ihm auch darin zuzustimmen, dass „damit das Recht auch anfällig für symbolische Vertrauenskrisen (ist)“[31]. Die Konstrukteure, vor allem aber die Dekonstrukteure Europas sollten dieser Gefahr ins Auge sehen. Doch sollten wir zugleich die von Michael Stolleis zuletzt aufgeworfene Frage, ob wir denn nicht zu hohe Erwartungen an das Recht stellen[32], ernsthaft diskutieren. Denn politische Dissense bedürfen einer politischen Antwort, die wir nicht an das Recht und die Gerichte abschieben können.

---

und damit ein Recht schafft, dass rechtlich nicht bindend ist, sondern als Empfehlung seine Wirkung entfalten soll. Doch die Forschung über die tatsächlichen Wirkungen steht noch am Anfang. Siehe dazu Kenneth W. ABBOTT/Duncan SNIDAL, Hard and Soft Law in International Governance, in: International Organization 54 (3) 2000, 421–456.

[31] Niklas LUHMANN (wie Anm. 4) 132.

[32] Michael STOLLEIS, Erwartungen an das Recht, in: Frankfurter Allgemeine Zeitung, 30.12.2003, Nr. 302, 7.